Better Than Homemade

Amazing Foods That Changed the Way We Eat

By Carolyn Wyman

QUIRK BOOKS
PHILADELPHIA

Library of Congress Cataloging in Publication Number: 2004100344

ISBN: 1-931686-42-4

Printed in Singapore

Typeset in Antique Olive, GillSans, Las Vegas Castaway

Designed by Michael Rogalski

A complete list of permission and trademark acknowledgments appears on page 138, which constitutes a continuation of this copyright page.

Distributed in North America by Chronicle Books
85 Second Street
San Francisco, CA 94105

10 9 8 7 6 5 4 3 2 1

Quirk Books
215 Church Street
Philadelphia, PA 19106
www.quirkbooks.com

For James and Viola Wyman,

the author's amazing inventors

Contents

4. Indestructibles and Recyclables 88
Foods for the long haul—plus recycled food-factory scraps

5. Marketing Marvels 112
Advertising has made these must-eats

Introduction

Computers and cell phones top most people's lists of the most important inventions of the twentieth century. My vote goes to Cheez Whiz. After all, what have computers and cell phones really done for us other than make it possible (and expected) to work 24/7? Processed foods, by contrast, have lessened the workload for millions while improving on Mother Nature's many shortcomings.

Cheez Whiz is a perfect example. Where cheddar and brie are strongly flavored and smelly and offer no consistency, every jar of Cheez Whiz has the same pleasing bland taste, from sea to shining sea, yesterday or the year it was invented (1953). Where regular cheese eventually grows disgusting green mold, an unopened jar of Cheez Whiz lasts practically forever (no refrigeration required!). Where making a cheese sauce requires considerable cooking skill, Cheez Whiz demands only the ability to open a jar.

Americans began taming their food in this way about the same time they tamed the West. The first cans of ground Folgers coffee were marketed as a convenience product to prospectors in the mining camps of the California Gold Rush fields. Premade condiments like Heinz Ketchup became commercially available as early as the late 1800s. Canned meat and vegetables have been on grocers' shelves even longer.

This book, however, focuses largely on a second—even more interesting—generation of convenience products created in the wake of World War II. It was a time when manufacturers desperate to unload the newfangled frozen, canned, and dried foods they had created for foxhole consumption found a willing population of women who had gone to work during the war, and who were no longer interested in fussing over meals.

Increased industrialization and, later, the Space Race created an uncritical fascination with technological innovation that made fake sugar, instant breakfast, shelf-stable snack cake, aerosol cheese, and powdered orange "drink" both technically possible and highly profitable. In the 1960s, serving a dinner of On-Cor Salisbury Steak and Gravy with instant mashed potatoes, canned peas, Pillsbury Crescent Rolls, and Hawaiian Punch was not just easier than making these things from scratch—it was also chic, the key to family happiness, and the right thing to do.

Who knew, then, that Mom was feeding her family near lethal doses of saturated fat and cholesterol? This was a time before the words "artificial flavoring" were hidden in ingredient lists instead of being proudly displayed in product names like 1956's Imitation Black Cherry Jell-O—before women were expected to hold full-time jobs and come

home to prepare wholesome meals from scratch with all-natural ingredients. If other advances in science and technology had experienced a similar backlash, we'd all be riding horses instead of driving cars and paying the iceman to deliver 50-pound blocks of ice instead of simply opening the freezer door.

The sad result? Most people today sneak-eat their favorite processed foods in guilt and shame. We know this because these foods that no one will admit eating are in fact some of America's best-selling brands. These sales are being made, in large part, to a whole generation of Americans who feel as nostalgic about Hamburger Helper, Kraft Macaroni & Cheese, and Little Debbie snack cakes as previous generations felt about Mom's meatloaf or pot roast or apple pie. In their homes, processed food *was* Mom's home cooking. (I was 12 before I discovered that vegetables came in some other form than cans or frozen blocks.)

We're buying these foods because they also taste good, in a predictable, pleasant way that is almost universally pleasing. Also because the name Tater Tots, the packaging of Jiffy Pop, and the advertising for Parkay are just plain fun (certainly a lot more so than any natural food store whole-grain cereal flakes).

This salute to some of America's greatest food innovations is specially formulated to be nostalgic, fun, and tasty. It's also fat- and calorie-free and, other than reading this introduction, no preparation is required.

Chapter 1

HOMEMAKER HELPERS

What's for dinner? For those who must answer that question long about 5 P.M. every day, no foods have been more prized than those in this chapter. They made getting dinner on the table quicker and easier and often with more delicious results than Mom could accomplish with a bunch of raw ingredients.

It's possible to live without Kraft Macaroni & Cheese and Marshmallow Fluff, but that sort of life just might not be worth living.

Birds Eye Frozen Vegetables
Fostering a Nation of Defrosters

Peeling the cardboard off a crystallized frozen block was a mid-twentieth-century dinner-making ritual. The peas and carrots or mixed vegetables that emerged from the pot 15 or 20 minutes later were so brightly colored they could have kept hunters safe from shooting accidents.

As scary as they looked, and as long as they took to cook (considerably longer than canned), these frozen veggie blocks were a godsend compared to the frozen foods that had been sold earlier in the century. Up till then, slow-freezing methods had produced

Inventor-adventurer Clarence Birdseye.

such bad-tasting and bad-looking food that many states required grocers to post warnings that they sold the so-called "cold storage" products. Consumers, duly informed, could then decide to take their patronage to less dubious establishments.

Enter Clarence Birdseye, an intrepid inventor-adventurer from Brooklyn. While on a fur-trading expedition to Labrador in 1912, Birdseye discovered that fresh fish and caribou meat froze almost immediately in the Arctic clime. When cooked up months later, the meat and fish were almost as tasty as fresh. Returning to New York, Birdseye dreamt of replicating this naturally occurring fast-freeze method.

Casting about for something to freeze, his eye landed on his son's ever-expanding collection of pet rabbits. (His wife must have been relieved they did not have a comparably large

We Would Have Switched Ad Agencies
Among the more memorable early ad lines for Birds Eye frosted foods:
Birds Eye fish:
  Frozen "with the wiggle in its tale."
Birds Eye spinach:
  "Washed, no sand!"

number of children.) With little more than some salt, some ice, some empty candy boxes, and a window fan, he froze rabbit, fish, and anything else he could get his hands on, and then invited friends and relatives over for taste tests. While the food was cooking, he would entertain his guests by bouncing frozen steaks on the floor.

With the financial backing of several partners, Birdseye opened a fish-freezing plant in the seacoast town of Gloucester, Massachusetts, in 1924. The plant featured a machine he had designed to simultaneously form and flash-freeze food into candy box–like rectangular blocks. "So whether it is a pound of lobster or a quart of strawberries it presents itself as a square hard brick, highly convenient to handle," enthused *Fortune* magazine.

But Birdseye's first retail packages of frozen food languished in warehouses. Consumers had no reason to think his frozen food would be any better than the old kind. Perhaps most critically, in his enthusiasm Birdseye had overlooked an essential fact: Few grocers and even fewer consumers owned freezers.

And then in 1925, a Birdseye goose laid a golden egg. Post cereal heiress Marjorie Post and her husband, E. F. Hutton (yes, that one), were cruising off the coast of Massachusetts in their yacht. One evening, their on-board chef served them a particularly delicious goose dinner. Aware that goose was out of season, Post asked the chef where he had gotten it. He explained that he had purchased it

A Birds Eye product "demonstrator" hard at work in Springfield, Mass., 1930.

If You Think the Stuff in the Far Reaches of Your Fridge Is Scary . . .
Frozen foods and nuclear bomb anxieties are firmly lodged in the American pop psyche. One piece of evidence: In the 1953 film *The Beast from 20,000 Fathoms*, a prehistoric monster that had been frozen for millions of years defrosts as the result of an atom bomb test, and then goes on a rampage through New York City. The beast destroys everything in its path—save the offices of the trade magazine *Quick Frozen Foods*.

frozen from a certain Mr. Birdseye. Intrigued, Post arranged a meeting with Clarence Birdseye and eventually convinced her husband and the Postum company's board of directors to buy the frozen foods company. Birdseye lent his name (split in two) and his technical expertise, and Postum invested in special packing plants, fishing trawlers, and insulated railroad cars.

In March 1930 Postum launched an initial line of 27 items (including peas, spinach, raspberries, chicken, steak, and haddock) at 18 supermarkets in Springfield, Massachusetts, with considerable fanfare and even greater expense. But four years later only 500 more stores were on board. In desperation, the company—now called General Foods—adopted a stealth approach: They sold the frozen foods to schools and hospitals, where the consumers wouldn't know what they were eating.

After years of languishing in relative anonymity, Birds Eye's retail market was revived by World War II. Women working in defense jobs didn't have time to make dinner from scratch, and with metal needed to make guns and tanks, canned foods were in short supply. Frozen foods also required fewer rationing points. Actually tasting the new frozen foods convinced consumers how much better they were than the old.

The results: Not only were more people eating frozen foods, but between 1920 and 1980 the amount of vegetables consumed in America doubled simply because so many more were available year-round. Like them or not, frozen vegetables meant a lot more vegetables eaten and a lot less rotting in fields or on store shelves.

In the 1930s, General Foods tried selling Birds Eye products through freezer dealers.

Minute Rice
Rice Be Perfect, Rice Be Quick

Nowadays if a man identifying himself as the son of an Afghan military chief and carrying a package big enough to contain a hot plate tried to drop in on an executive at any major American food corporation, he'd probably be out the door in a minute (or detained for hours). But the world was a simpler place in 1941.

That's when Ataullah Durrani waltzed unannounced into the Manhattan office of a General Foods executive. He whipped out some cooking equipment, then whipped up a pot of delicious white, fluffy rice in only a fraction of the typical half-hour cooking time. His secret? He used pre-cooked grains. Although it turned out Durrani could not replicate a pan of rice this good any more consistently than most housewives, General Foods was intrigued with the idea of developing a quick-cooking rice companion to their already successful Minute Tapioca.

The company quickly set their scientists to work on the consistency problem and even retrofitted part of their Hoboken, New Jersey, plant as a rice laboratory—until the U.S. Army requisitioned it for the war effort in 1942. The same thing happened the next year

The only rice that comes out of the box pre-cooked!

... and the only one that gives you **perfect rice without cooking!**

An exclamation point–filled ad from 1956.

Unauthorized Use

Some home brewers make light beer by tossing Minute Rice in with their malt. (Regular rice apparently won't work nearly as well.)

with their second rice plant in Battle Creek, Michigan.

The government, as it happened, wanted General Foods' new quick-cooking rice for soldiers' C rations even before the tedious research on optimal cooking times and moisture content could be completed. (How tedious was it? To determine dryness, the scientists had to count the holes in individual rice grains—which is about as close as you can get to counting angels on the head of a pin.) So soldiers were the first guinea pigs for the consumer Minute Rice that rolled out in supermarkets across the country between 1946 and 1949.

Its debut was heralded by an unprecedented advertising and promotional blitz. "Amazing New Rice Discovery Makes Dazzling Dishes a Cinch to Prepare!" one early ad boasted. "No washing! No rinsing! No draining! No steaming!" "Just boil water. That's the hard part," another ad joked. "Add Minute Rice. Do not cook."

Six women representing the world's leading rice-producing countries beautified the product's launch in New York, and in New Orleans salesmen were treated to a visit from International Rice Queen Mary Alice Toso.

No wonder initial sales were strong. But they dropped off quickly—and this also probably should not have come as a

surprise. In the 1940s, rice was this meat-and-potatoes nation's mealtime starch only 10 percent of the time. To boost that number, General Foods launched a second ad campaign featuring recipes for "dream dishes" and "swifty nifties" like Drumsticks and Chili Rice (Minute Rice seasoned with chili powder served with drumsticks shaped out of hamburger) and Bacon 'n Egg Rice (breakfast over rice topped with melted Velveeta). For women who got home late from bridge club, the company offered a "Magic Rice Dinner Plan" involving leftover pork, frozen broccoli, mock Hollandaise sauce, and (of course) Minute Rice.

"I'm too busy" or unskilled to make real rice—in ad after ad, General Foods rode these two themes and the "Perfect Rice Every Time" kicker to sales dominance. By the late '50s, Minute Rice was the best-selling rice in the land. And it stayed that way through much of the next two decades.

By all rights Minute Rice should be even more popular now that Americans are busier and by and large less cooking literate. Instead, it has been largely surpassed in the trendy starch sweepstakes by couscous (which naturally cooks in Minute Rice's five minutes), and it is rivaled in convenience by the rice cooker, which many believe produces even more perfect rice every time.

He Gave Us 15 Years to Save Us 15 Minutes

Ataullah Durrani gave up his position as a member of Afghanistan's ruling family and forfeited a glamorous life of Hollywood parties to bring the world instant rice.

Although he was cousin to the Afghan king and the son of its military leader, Durrani left his native land in the early 1920s to study chemistry in America. One night while entertaining the future president of the American Can Company, he hit upon his research subject: a technique for cooking and then canning the delicious rice from his homeland.

In 1934, Durrani moved to Hollywood to serve as a consultant on movies set in the "exotic" East and earn money for his canning experiments. His royal status and delicious rice dinners got him invited to all the best parties. But his heart was with his experiments. By 1939 he had earned enough to move to Arkansas, the heart of American rice country. It was there that he came up with the breakthrough idea of *drying* the cooked rice and selling it in boxes instead of in heavy and expensive-to-ship cans. And soon he was knocking on General Foods' door.

"Rice-Ipes" pamphlet from the early '90s.

On-Cor Family-Size Entrees
Cheaper by the Trayful

TV dinners are seen as downscale in some circles, but try serving them to a family of five every day of the week and they'll begin to seem downright pricey.

That's where On-Cor comes in. For consumers who are too busy (or incompetent) to make Hamburger Helper, these huge trays of meat "patties" and gravy seem heaven-sent.

On-Cor was a Chicago-area purveyor of frozen sliced meat and sandwiches before 1958, when owner Sol Friend decided to create the first family-sized frozen entrée. Since then, the company has stuck to its trademark two-pound frozen main dish like the On-Cor breading on their veal parmigiana.

Every day one breaded and one unbreaded entrée is made at On-Cor's Fort Atkinson, Wisconsin, plant. Visit on a day when their best-selling Salisbury steak and gravy entrée is being made and you'll see workers placing raw meat onto a conveyor leading to a grinder. Once ground, the meat is placed in a blending tank with spices and seasonings. After blending, a forming machine spits the meat out onto a conveyor belt as patties. The patties then pass through a stainless steel tunnel where they're actually flame-broiled. From there the steaks are frozen, then shipped to the company's Chicago plant to be united with their gravy in a customized metal tray.

That's the On-Cor consumers don't see. Over the years, the public face of On-Cor has included an On-Cor puppet made by Jim Henson, just-folks celebrities Stiller and Meara, and Al Molinaro, who played the malt shop owner on TV's *Happy Days*. Trading on his association with straight-ahead American eats, Molinaro plays a grocer who is always trying to invite himself over for dinner to help people polish off their On-Cor in spots that emphasize the meals' huge size.

Today, On-Cor remains the only line of value-priced, family-sized frozen entrées that still delivers two pounds of food. Whereas copycat competitors Banquet and Freezer Queen went to 28 ounces years ago—in a nod to their bottom lines and lighter eating trends—On-Cor's only lasting concession to lighter eating has been the introduction of entrées such as turkey with dressing, sweet and sour chicken and rice, and chicken breast tenders with spaghetti, where part of the poundage comes from a starch. But On-Cor executives tout them mainly in terms of their greater convenience: "Instead of just cooking up the entrée, now the consumer doesn't have to cook the noodles as well," points out current company president Howard Friend.

Consumers trade up to restaurants and Stouffer's in good times, but On-Cor sells best in bad. To make up for their recession-sensitive supermarket market, the company sells some of its meat patties, chicken nuggets, and meatballs to food service. Should they ever tire of their "Taste and More" slogan, "On-Cor: We bring the cafeteria food home" wouldn't be a bad substitute.

Chicago children's TV personality Frazier Thomas and Garfield Goose touted the 20,000 rubber ducky premiums mailed to On-Cor consumers in the '50s.

The mascot for On-Cor's Redi-Serve food service division.

Wyman's Believe It or Not

Noodles and sauces in On-Cor frozen meals are all made from scratch. In fact, the company changed its slogan from the fill-'er-up "When you want more, it's On-Cor" to the quality-oriented "For taste and more, it's On-Cor" in 1989, precisely for this reason.

Hamburger Helper
Help for the Ground Beef–Challenged

Dessert kits that debuted with Jell-O at the turn of the century had grown to a full supermarket baking aisle by the 1950s, but consumers had to wait until 1971 to enjoy the convenience of a main meal kit.

"One pan, one pound [of hamburger], one box—one happy family," declared the introductory ads for Hamburger Helper, boxes of premeasured dry starch and sauce powders in stroganoff, hash, chili, beef noodle, and Oriental rice flavors.

Cookbooks from the 1970s are filled with recipes for just this same kind of bland glop. But to make them consumers actually had to find a recipe and buy and measure out all the ingredients—whereas in ease and idiotproofness (as well as aesthetics) Hamburger Helper rivaled paint-by-number kits. Hamburger Helper dinner mix was also cheap (59 cents), quick (20 minutes), and could stretch a pound of hamburger into a main meal for five at a time when beef prices were at an all-time high. In fact, helping consumers manage meat prices was the product's main impetus when it debuted.

Consumers ate up Hamburger Helper in huge numbers, prompting new Cheeseburger Macaroni and Lasagna flavors and the spinoff Tuna Helper and Fruit Helper lines (in 1972 and 1973, respectively). When beef prices declined and sales stalled in the late 1970s, the brand got assistance from a cartoon helping hand. He dressed up like an Italian waiter to introduce Zesty and Cheesy Italian flavors in 1989. Later, the Helping Hand put a funnel on its thumb to pass itself off as a chicken and presumably get Mom thinking about mixing up some tasty Chicken Helper (which bowed in 1984 and then was retooled and reintroduced in 1991 and again in 1998).

The Bottom of a Pretty Deep Advertising Well

Of course it makes sense that people in the image-generating business of advertising would rather work on a hip brand like ESPN *SportsCenter* than a dowdy one like Tide. But advertising copywriter Ginger MacDonald says Hamburger Helper is the most dreaded brand of all.

"No writer wanted it on his or her resume that he was responsible for the Helping Hand wearing a sombrero while singing a jingle about Cheesy Taco Bake," notes MacDonald, who, in fact, can claim just such a credit.

For almost 20 years, General Mills kept that (probably too) literal symbol of the Helping Hand on the pulse of pot-luck cooking trends, introducing Cheesy Hashbrowns, Cheesy Nacho, Double Cheese Pizza, Fettuccine Alfredo, Philly Cheese, Cheesy Shells, and Cheesy Enchilada—Hamburger Helper food scientists' favorite way of helping hamburger apparently involving cheese. Their one attempt to serve gourmets—Macaroni Newburg Tuna Helper containing "a hint of wine"—was discontinued in 1978.

The media elite had long scoffed at Hamburger Helper (the most famous example being the scene in *National Lampoon's Vacation* where the hopelessly cheap Randy Quaid serves Hamburger Helper without the hamburger), but in a 2001 *Wall Street Journal* article, it was Helper executives who were scoffing at the new competition from "meat-complete" frozen meal kits such as Stouffer's Skillet Sensations and Green Giant Complete Skillet Meals. The new competition didn't require enough "involvement" to assuage the guilt consumers felt about using convenience products, one General Mills executive told the *Journal*. "People are obsessed with meat" and do not want large food companies choosing it for them, added another.

Only a few months later, however, and despite their higher cost, Banquet Homestyle Bakes meal kits, complete with canned meat, were burning up checkout scanners, and Helper executives were eating their words along with their hamburger. Suddenly the disembodied clown's hand was back after a seven-year hiatus, in a new TV ad campaign courting the brand's typical customer: a married female homemaker with three-plus kids, a Ford Escort, a household income of under $35,000, and merited insecurity about her cooking abilities.

Laugh at Hamburger Helper if you want, but it is probably the best thing this woman's family gets to eat all week.

Like most cartoon hands, Hamburger Helper's Helping Hand has only four fingers.

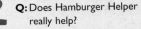

Pop Question

Q: Does Hamburger Helper really help?

A: General Mills has spent 30 years and millions of dollars to make Hamburger Helper sound like the inept chef's best friend. But the Hamburger Helper FAQ on the Betty Crocker Web site makes it sound like a culinary train wreck. Why aren't the noodles or potatoes fully cooked, so dry, so wet, so soft, so chewy, or so gummy? are just a few of the questions there addressed. These questions and their carefully described correctives should send the target audience of insecure cooks running, screaming, to the nearest McDonald's.

Kraft Macaroni & Cheese
Comfort in a Cardboard Carton

Sing, Duck; Sing, Duck
It's been more than a decade since the Canadian pop group Barenaked Ladies first promised that they would still eat Kraft Dinner even "If I Had $1,000,000." And for more than a decade, the group has been pelted by bone-hard pasta, orange cheese powder, and occasionally even unopened Kraft Dinner boxes at their live concerts. To show their public-mindedness— and perhaps spare themselves some pain in the process—the band now stations food bank collection boxes at their concert venues.

It's cheap, keeps nearly a year without refrigeration, and is quick and easy to make while still demanding enough to make you feel like you're cooking. (Most people claim their own trademark "improvement" on the package instructions.) It's bland enough to appeal to all palates and to allow for the incorporation of many other ingredients (vegetables, hot dogs, tuna, and ground beef being among the most popular).

Could Kraft Macaroni & Cheese Dinner (a.k.a. Kraft Dinner, Blue Box, or Vitamin K) be North America's most perfect convenience food? In Canada it's the number-one-selling grocery item and an object of worship on par with hockey.

You might assume that such a work of processed food genius was the multiyear effort of dozens of food marketing and technical whizzes. In fact, however, it was the creation of a now-forgotten salesman for the Tenderoni Macaroni company of St. Louis who found his product easier to unload with packets of Kraft grated cheese attached. When Kraft got wind, they hired the salesman to promote the idea. Kraft introduced his product nationally in a yellow box in 1937. (It didn't gain its iconic blue hue until the 1950s.)

Most Americans had at least heard of macaroni and cheese—after trying it in France, Thomas Jefferson introduced it to the New World as a sidelight to founding the country—but it was only really popular in the South. (It's still the standard accompaniment to fried chicken and collard greens there.) But Kraft had the Depression on its side. At 19 cents for four servings, Kraft Dinner was an instant success, selling 8 million boxes in its first year. Ease and speed of preparation were Kraft's major selling points. "How the deuce did you make this keen macaroni and cheese so fast? Why, we just got home!" a hungry husband enthused in one early ad.

World War II provided another boon for the brand. Because Kraft Macaroni & Cheese was considered a good substitute for scarce fresh meat and dairy, two boxes required only one rationing coupon. That boosted sales to 80 million boxes in 1943. Today Kraft sells about 350 million boxes annually in the United States alone.

Kraft Mac & Cheese has long been a staple of the young and the budget-conscious. Food writer Cathy Barber called its neon orange the beacon that guides kids to the dinner table. Kids' natural affinity for the food is aided and abetted by an aggressive program of kid-oriented advertising and marketing Kraft has pursued since the late 1980s, including a whole series of limited-edition Kraft Dinners with macaroni shaped like favorite cartoon characters. Over the years Bugs Bunny, the Flintstones, Scooby-Doo, and SpongeBob SquarePants have all ended up in hot water.

In the '90s adults got Kraft Dinner versions of white cheddar, three cheese, and Alfredo restaurant pasta dishes. The comfort-food trend at the turn of the twenty-first century produced $25 macaroni

The Cheesiest

Kraft Canada's 1998 search for the country's biggest Kraft Dinner fan unearthed a Saskatchewan bachelor farmer who wolfs down up to 800 boxes a year. Wes Gidluck was understandably disappointed by a top prize that included only 365 boxes. "I guess they figured that was a year's supply, but I thought it was a little on the chintzy side," said Gidluck, who also hoped aloud that the publicity might yield him a wife who could boil (lots of) water.

Wait till you taste *this* macaroni-and-cheese! And I'll have it ready in a "jif"!

7 minutes . . .

A twinkling

THE BEST MACARONI-AND-CHEESE I'VE EVER TASTED!

COOKING TIME only *7 minutes*

KRAFT DINNER

Busy working gals were the target of many ads when "Blue Box" was mainly yellow (i.e., in the early 1940s).

Some (lazy?) economists gauge U.S. economic health via the Kraft Macaroni & Cheese Index, a simple tracking of sales of this classic recession food. That's right, Alan Greenspan is *not* a KD fan.

and cheese dishes on upscale restaurant menus. Mark Peel of the L.A. restaurant Campanile told the *Los Angeles Times* in 2002: "You can do a lot of things with [macaroni and cheese], though you have to have one foot in tradition." In other words, the box is in our collective solar plexus; chefs ignore this at their peril.

Cajun Comfort (with Italian Seasoning)

In 2002 Kraft capitalized on the from-scratch gourmet macaroni and cheese phenomenon by commissioning New Orleans (and TV) chef Emeril Lagasse to create this upscale recipe using good old Blue Box, with a little help from its sister product, Velveeta.

$1/2$ pound smoked sausage, casing removed, finely chopped
1 teaspoon minced garlic
1 pound boneless, skinless chicken breasts, cut into 1-inch cubes
$1/2$ cup chopped onion
$1/4$ cup chopped celery
$1/4$ cup chopped green pepper
1 teaspoon salt
$1/2$ teaspoon black pepper
1 14.5-ounce can crushed tomatoes
6 cups water
1 14.5-ounce family-size box or 2 7.25-ounce boxes Kraft Macaroni & Cheese Dinner
1 teaspoon Italian seasoning
$1/4$ cup butter or margarine
1 cup milk
$1/4$ pound Velveeta, cut into cubes

Heat a 12-inch nonstick sauté pan on medium-high heat. Add sausage to pan; cook 3 minutes, stirring constantly. Add garlic and chicken; cook 3 minutes, stirring frequently. Add onion, celery, and green pepper. Season with salt and pepper. Cook 3 minutes. Add tomatoes; cook 5 minutes, stirring occasionally.

Meanwhile, bring 6 cups water to a boil in a 2-quart stockpot. Add macaroni to boiling water; cook 7 to 10 minutes or until tender, stirring occasionally. Drain macaroni. Add to ingredients in sauté pan along with Italian seasoning. Stir in Kraft Dinner cheese sauce packet, butter, milk, and Velveeta. Cook 5 minutes, or until cut-up cheese is melted and mixture is thickened, stirring frequently. Serves 8.

Kraft Dinner's second special pasta shape, Wheels, debuted in 1988 and were renamed the more exciting "Wild Wheels" in 1991.

Potato Buds
Instant Mashed Potatoes
This Spud's a Bud

Peeling potatoes is the worse kind of time-consuming grunt work and, believe it or not, one of the main reasons women didn't have time to work outside the home until after World War II—when instant mashed potatoes were invented.

Although a number of companies had been feverishly working on the instant mashed "problem," R.T. French company of London was the first to take out a U.S. patent on the process in 1946, and they were the first to make them here. The Rendle method of making instant mashed—named for the British scientist who developed it for a French's affiliate—involved adding previously dried potato granules to some cooked and mashed potatoes before drying to produce granules that could be reconstituted with hot water or milk.

French's pretty much had the instant mashed potato market to itself until the mid-1950s, when a new and much simpler method for making instant mashed was developed by government scientists in Philadelphia to deal with a postwar potato surplus. By this method the cooked mashed potato is dried in sheets that are then broken apart to form flakes. The new "Philadelphia cook"

Instant Mashed in Every Pot
Any smart political consultant with access to Claritas Inc. market research data would advise the next Republican presidential candidate to buy some space on the back of a Potato Buds package. That research shows instant mashed potato eaters to be even more politically conservative than fans of red meat.

New from Betty Crocker
Instant Mashed Potatoes

Instant mashed potatoes became part of Betty Crocker's cooking repertoire in 1959.

"Hello!" "Goodbye"

Betty Crocker has taken her best instant mashed potatoes off the market to make room for something even better: 'Potato Buds' — instant mashed potatoes in a totally new form — not flakes, not granules, but tiny puffs of real Idaho potatoes that blossom into mashed potatoes better tasting than any others — even homemade.

Betty Crocker Instant Mashed got the hook in 1965.

method didn't require the extra step of adding back dried potato granules and also could be successfully made with virtually any potato variety (unlike Rendle's, which required Idahos).

The Philadelphia cook spawned many competitive instant potato products, including one from General Mills spokeswoman Betty Crocker. "Perfect mashed potatoes every time! Won't lump, can't lump!" Betty's early ads boasted. "Fresh potato flavor and texture in a quick potato that is creamy, mealy and rich" (mealiness then apparently being seen as a desirable quality).

In 1965, however, General Mills decided to dump Betty in favor of the new and far superior Potato Buds brand. "Not flakes, not granules, but tiny puffs of real Idaho potatoes that blossom into mashed potatoes better tasting than any others, even homemade," explained an ad that showed the new Potato Buds box bumping an old Betty Crocker Mashed right off the page.

In its heyday in the '50s and the '60s, instant mashed was the glue that held family dinners together—literally so in the case of popular dishes such as shepherd's pie, hot dog casserole, and igloo meat loaf (made by mounding the meat and frosting it with the potatoes). Although some said it also tasted like glue, most homemakers of the time would no more think of making mashed potatoes from scratch than they would think of pulling out a washboard to wash clothes.

In the '70s and '80s, however, instant mashed potatoes were one of those "magic powder foods" (like Lipton Onion Soup Mix, Tang, and Jell-O) that fell out of favor as "off trend" in face of consumer demand for less processed foods. Poor sales drove even pioneer French's from the market.

Instant mashed potatoes are still popular with middle-class families with children, according to an executive with rival instant mashed brand Hungry Jack, who in a 1997 *Wall Street Journal* article characterized them as "a nice gut-filler."

Even people who wouldn't be caught dead with a box of Potato Buds or Hungry Jack in their cupboard probably eat them more often than they realize, especially if they frequent cafeterias and fast food restaurants like KFC (also the country's leading ambassador of instant mashed to the rest of the world).

Premium Edition Potato Buds

A popular Internet recipe for improving the taste of instant mashed potatoes that takes about as long to make as real mashed. (Yes, it's crazy. And that's why we love it.)

2 2/3 cups Potato Buds mashed potato flakes
2/3 cup milk
1 8-ounce package cream cheese
2 tablespoons green onion, chopped
1 tablespoon butter
Paprika
2 tablespoons fresh or 1 tablespoon dried parsley

Preheat oven to 400°F. Prepare Potato Buds with milk according to package directions, but use the cream cheese in place of the called-for butter or margarine. Stir in green onion. Place in 1-quart baking dish. Dot with butter and sprinkle with paprika and parsley. Bake 30 minutes or until heated all the way through. Serves 6.

Hot Dog Casserole

1 1/3 cups water
1/3 cup milk
2 tablespoons butter or margarine
1/2 teaspoon salt
1 1/3 cups Potato Buds mashed potato flakes
1/4 cup sweet pickle relish
2 tablespoons mayonnaise or salad dressing
1 tablespoon instant minced onion
2 teaspoons yellow mustard
4 to 6 hot dogs

Heat oven to 350°F. Heat water, milk, butter, and salt to boiling in a 2-quart saucepan. Remove from heat. Stir in dry potatoes until just moist. Let stand about 30 seconds or until liquid is absorbed. Whip with fork until fluffy. Stir in relish, mayonnaise, onion, and mustard. Spread in ungreased 1-quart casserole.

Cut each hot dog in half lengthwise and crosswise. Arrange hot dog pieces around edge of mashed potatoes. Bake uncovered 25 to 30 minutes or until center is hot. Serves 3 to 4.

Unauthorized Use

Soothe a burn or bite with a paste made by combining a little bit of Potato Buds flakes with water. Potato Buds flakes can also be used to thicken soups, gravies, and even real mashed potatoes to which you've added too much milk.

Marshmallow Fluff
A Sticky Business

A pile of Fluffernutters from the *Yummy* cookbook.

Almost by definition, fluff is not something anyone needs. And yet when Marshmallow Fluff was invented in the early 1900s, it represented a giant leap forward in the evolution of white, sugary treats. Regular marshmallows with their powdery coating are fairly neat and discrete but must be melted for use in most recipes. But there's nowhere you can't use Marshmallow Fluff, and there's nothing that it can't turn into a sweet sticky mess. Mud pies are clean by comparison.

Marshmallow Fluff debuted in grocery stores in 1917 as Toot Sweet Marshmallow Fluff. The first two words were a pun on *tout de suite,* the French term for "quick," but when it became apparent that nobody else got the joke, candymakers H. Allen Durkee and Fred Mower got rid of it.

The product was peddled door-to-door even earlier by Archibald Query, a salesman who sold the pair the recipe for $500. That might sound like a steep price for four ingredients (corn syrup, sugar, dried egg white, and vanilla flavoring), but H. Allen's son, Don, says, "It's the whipping and cooking time, the manipulation of the ingredients that makes Fluff unique." And sticky: The daily washdown of plant walls and floors takes one-and-a-half hours.

Durkee-Mower is one of only two U.S. companies that still make marshmallow crème, and it's the only one that makes it in small batches, producing "a consistency which . . . a continuous batch process can't ever equal," according to the company's Web site PR fluffery.

Fluff is whipped in 80-pound vats then hand-fed into a chute that feeds into a bottling machine. The jars it fills are almost as important to sales as the Fluff itself. In the late 1940s, the jar was redesigned to make it better for storing food leftovers of all kinds. The label design—of a spoonful of Fluff resembling a cloud floating against a light blue background resembling a sky—also hasn't changed for decades.

The most popular use for Fluff is on white bread with peanut butter to create that school lunchbox classic the Fluffernutter sandwich. Fluff's most popular recipe is for Never-Fail Fudge. The company's *Yummy* cookbook (which can be purchased on a 2004 Web server for the 1950s price of $1) also contains crème adaptations for such marshmallow favorites as Rice Krispies Treats, Whoopie Pies, and really sweet Sweet Potato Casserole, along with modern innovations like Fluff smoothies—made by combining 1 cup juice, 3 ice cubes, and 2 heaping tablespoons Marshmallow Fluff in a blender. (Just thinking about this drink can make your teeth ache.)

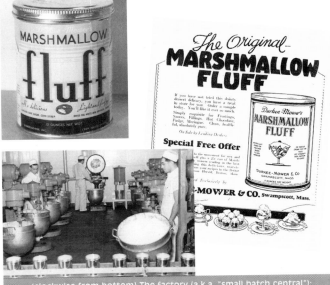

(clockwise from bottom) The factory (a.k.a. "small batch central"); the can it produced in the early 1940s; an early ad from the 1920s.

Q: My Never-Fail Fudge failed. Why?

A: This Frequently Asked Question from the Fluff Web site is yet more proof of the sorry state of cooking literacy in contemporary America.

The standard answer? You probably didn't let the fudge cook long enough or at a high enough temperature. Fair warning should you want to try the following recipe.

2½ cups sugar
¾ teaspoon salt
½ stick butter or margarine
1 5.33-ounce can evaporated milk
1 7.5-ounce jar Marshmallow Fluff
¾ teaspoon vanilla
1 12-ounce bag semi-sweet chocolate pieces
½ cup walnuts, chopped

Grease a 9-inch square baking pan; set aside. In a large saucepan, combine first 5 ingredients. Stir over low heat until blended. Heat to a full boil, being careful not to mistake escaping air bubbles for boiling. Boil slowly, stirring constantly, for 5 minutes. Remove from heat; stir in vanilla and chocolate until chocolate is melted. Add nuts. Turn into greased pan and cool. Makes 2½ pounds.

Shake 'n Bake
Tase-tee Frahd Cheeken—Without Frahen!

The set-up was standard: a child helping Mom in the kitchen. The soundtrack was not.

"It's not frahd," the little girl boasted in one of the first (and only) national ads to feature strong Southern accents. "It's Shike 'n Bike—an' Ah hepped!"

If this was not the most annoying commercial in television history, it is certainly in

New Shake 'n Bake makes crispy golden chicken without frying!

Complete! Coating mix and a shaker bag! You get lightly seasoned coating mix and a handy shaker bag. Pour the mix into the bag—there's enough for 2½ pounds of chicken.

Just add chicken! Moisten each piece of chicken with water or milk, then drop it into the shaker bag. It is large enough to hold two or three pieces of chicken at a time.

Shake...and bake! Each piece of chicken is evenly covered with coating mix ...turns crispy golden right in your oven. No messy frying, no hot fat! Clean up? Throw the bag away.

Perfect chicken with real country flavor! Crisp golden chicken, lightly seasoned with herbs and spices, with all the delicious juices sealed in. For perfect chicken, try new Shake 'n Bake!

Good Seasons There's a Shake 'n Bake for Fish, too...no frying, no fishy smell!

Debut ads (like this one from 1965) mixed equal parts instruction and enthusiasm.

the top 10. Certainly it's enough to send the blood pressure of anyone who watched TV in the mid-'60s (or the mid-'70s, when it was revived with a pair of Southern twins) soaring. And yet Shake 'n Bake survived to see many more decades. The less controversial introductory print ads and promotional materials explain why.

"No batter to mix, no mess to clean up. Chicken's ready for the oven in 5 minutes!" screamed one 1965 ad that outlined the three-step process: pouring the powder into the plastic bag, placing a water-moistened chicken leg in the bag, and shaking. At the time, Kentucky Fried Chicken was sweeping the nation. But frying food at home was a messy and scary business, especially for Northern and Western housewives whose moms

Most Popular Riddle with a Shake 'n Bake Punchline

What happens when you cross an earthquake with a fire?

had never taught them how. Shake 'n Bake's combination of flour, oil, sugar, mustard, onion, beet, caramel (for color), and secret herbs and spices offered "a new way to prepare crispy golden chicken or fish without frying"—and without its sure mess or potential to burn.

Although the early ads didn't mention it, making the chicken fly around in the bag was almost as much fun as throwing pizza dough in the air, but so much easier that even a child could do it. In fact, the phenomenon of kids "hepping" is still a significant factor in Shake 'n Bake sales.

By 1979, however, even General Foods had had enough of the Southerners. They were replaced by the Ann Landers of meat troubles, a butcher named Pete who advised women plagued by tough chicken or dry pork chops to (surprise!) buy Shake 'n Bake. Ads from the 1980s and 1990s focused on new flavors or recipe ideas—that is, until 1994, when the company decided to bring the original Southern girl back to introduce Shake 'n Bake's new Perfect Potatoes seasonings mixes for fresh potatoes.

Part of a 1997 ad that continued the kids "hepping" theme.

To be more precise, it was a black-and-white video image of her dropped onto a color ad of a contemporary family à la *Forrest Gump* and *The Twilight Zone*. Sales rose 9 percent—which only goes to show how much people are attracted to the familiar, even when it's reviled.

Not to be Confused With
- summertime political candidate meet-and-greet events
- combination fitness and tanning centers
- emergency firefighter shelters
- boxer Vaughn Bean
- when a basketball player avoids an opponent to sink a shot
- an important algorithm for determining molecular structures

—all of which are also called shake 'n bake.

Kool-Aid
Sweet? Inexpensive? Oh, yeah!

Sure, fruit juice is more nutritious. But most families would go bankrupt if they fed their thirsty kids 100-percent juice all summer long. And what kid will drink plain water? For the past three-quarters of a century, Kool-Aid has kept kids hydrated while keeping families financially solvent. The first ads said, "5 cents makes 10 big, cool glasses." The Internet-age price is less than a nickel a glass.

If Kool-Aid had been around when Edwin Perkins was a kid, he would have had a Kool-Aid stand—no question. Instead, in 1900, at age 11, he responded to an ad at the back of a magazine that read, "Be a manufacturer—Mixer's Guide tells how—write." He proceeded to take over his mother's Hendley, Nebraska, kitchen, making perfumes, patent medicines, and other concoctions.

Perkins's products grew into Perkins Products, a Hastings, Nebraska, company that used the Onor-Maid brand name and by the mid-1920s sold more than 125 products, including a liquid drink concentrate called Fruit Smack. Fruit Smack showed great promise, but its glass bottles were plagued by leakage and breakage. So Perkins hired a chemist to turn the concentrate into a powder he called Kool-Aid (borrowing the hyphen and the "aid" from his brand's name), which he sold in 1-ounce packets for 10 cents (but soon lowered to 5 cents). It was 1927, just before the Great Depression ruined many businesses and sealed Kool-Aid's success.

Packets of unsweetened Kool-Aid cost 5 cents for more than 20 years, until shortly after inventor Edwin Perkins sold the business to General Foods. General Foods—or more specifically its ad agency's art director—came up with the

Cry No More for Sharkleberry

Members of the Kool-Aid Usenet group offer instructions for recreating defunct flavors with combinations of existing ones. For instance, Sharkleberry Fin can be made by mixing $1/2$ teaspoon each of unsweetened Lemonade, Orange, and Strawberry flavors of Kool-Aid, 1 cup of sugar, and $1/2$ gallon of water. For Sunshine Punch, mix equal amounts of sugar-sweetened Orange- and Lemonade-flavored Kool-Aid with $1/2$ gallon of water.

In this 1949 ad, Kool-Aid is as cooling as a huge waterfall.

brand's trademark smiling pitcher. Marvin Potts thought up this way of communicating the summertime drink's cool refreshment when he saw his son drawing pictures on a frosty window-pane in the winter of 1954.

For a long time on TV the pitcher did nothing more than sit around in the fridge smiling and singing, "Kool-Aid, Kool-Aid—tastes great! Kool-Aid, Kool-Aid, can't wait!" But by 1975 the pitcher had sprouted arms and legs: A new superhero persona was born in a series of ads where he literally broke down walls to deliver Kool-Aid to kids screaming, "Hey Kool-Aid!"

Without fail, Kool-Aid Man's inarticulate response was always, "Oh, yeahhh!" Kool-Aid Man never apologized or explained the reason he didn't enter buildings through doors like other, more civilized pitchers (although the reasonable assumption was that he was high on Kool-Aid sugar).

By the 1980s, Kool-Aid Man had begun to channel that energy into more constructive activities, including skateboarding, beach volleyball, mountain climbing, go-cart racing, hiking, in-line skating, playing guitar, and singing hip-hop. After years of wearing the same old striped shirt, jeans, and sneakers, he also began dressing better—wearing hiking shorts and boots on the Mega Mountain Twist flavor packets and a swimsuit for the best-selling

STIR UP A PITCHERFUL OF FUN!

Kool-Aid

5¢ package makes **two** quarts

9 Great Flavors including NEW LEMON! Try 'em all!

Kool-Aid Man as he appeared in 1956—long before he started breaking down walls.

Tropical Punch, although why he wore a cowboy outfit on the Raspberry remains a mystery.

The product itself has kept up with the times with new forms and flavors. Kids who spend their summer at day camp can tote along already-made Kool-Aid Jammers; there are now Tamarindo, Mandarina Tangerine, and Jamaica flavors with bilingual packaging as well as Magic Twist varieties that change colors and taste different than they look (thus making the already hard job of identifying Kool-Aid flavors well nigh impossible).

Defunct flavors like Raspberry (Perkins's favorite), Root Beer, Golden Nectar, Pineapple-Grapefruit, and Sharkleberry Fin (whatever that was) are mourned by members of the Kool-Aid Usenet group (alt.drink.kool-aid). Its FAQ says Great Bluedini

Unauthorized Uses

Kool-Aid was the medium for LSD delivery for writer Ken Kesey and the Merry Pranksters, as described in 1968's *The Electric Kool Aid Acid Test* by Tom Wolfe.

In the mid-'90s, Kool-Aid became popular as a cheap, relatively benign way for teenage punks to dye their hair primary-school colors. "It gives me a mad, happy feeling," a Lemon-Lime–haired Ron Dow, 15, told the *Wall Street Journal* before a rainstorm cut the interview short. (Dow reappeared later in the story with a green nose and cheeks.)

Stuffed into a showerhead or scattered in a fountain, Kool-Aid also makes a good practical joke. (But you didn't hear it from us.)

1930

1956

was discontinued for fear little kids would confuse it with Windex and wind-shield washer fluid. (The company says it was just in the normal course of flavor rotation and that they now sell a similar Berry Blue.)

In the 1960s and again in 1986, a premium program featuring kites, dolls, and video games advertising Kool-Aid Man sweetened the already sweet drink. An old *Adventures of Kool-Aid Man* comic book that once went for four proofs-of-purchase now fetches $5 on the Internet—less than you would think, considering that its cover features one of the only known authorized depictions of Kool-Aid Man frowning (because the warm-weather–loving Scorch stole a giant key, if you must know).

You can learn more at the "Discover the Dream" exhibit at the Hastings Museum in Hastings, Nebraska, the town where Kool-Aid was born. It features a fiber-optic river of Kool-Aid as well as a theater where people can watch Kool-Aid ads with no non-commercial interruptions. Hastings also hosts an annual Kool-Aid Festival in August featuring the world's largest Kool-Aid stand (75 feet long). In other words, Kool-Aid is turning stodgy Nebraska into a vacation destination. Talk about break-ing down walls. Oh, yeah!

Ethnic Mix

Like many fruity-sweet American drinks and desserts, Kool-Aid skews high in ethnic markets (which is food brand–speak for African-Americans and Hispanics). The Kool-Aid that is sold in Latin America (and has been since Day 1—Edwin Perkins was clearly a demographic visionary) is even sweeter than the one sold in the United States, if you can imagine it.

Kraft began to pursue the Asian-American market after learning of Asian-American mothers' concerns about carbonated drinks—specifically their fears that "the bubbles filled the stomach and left little room for nutri-tious food," as reported in the June 14, 1993, *Brandweek* magazine. Sensing an opening for a non-carbonated soft drink that was fortified with vitamin C, Kraft retained Asian ad agency Muse Cordero Chen—and thus the "Happy, Happy, Happy" advertising campaign was launched. "A happy drink means a happy youth" was the message that ultimately reached 60 percent of the Asian-American mar-ket, or double the campaign's goal, according to *Brandweek*.

1970   1979   1991

DINTY MOORE Beef Stew
A Man's Can

<Nowadays people who don't have the time or skill to cook dinner can have McDonald's or a TV dinner. But for many years their best friend was Dinty Moore Beef Stew.

If you believed Dinty Moore advertising from the 1960s and '70s, the stew was made by a lumberjack named Dinty Moore, who got

Hunters Stew Tip...

DINTY MOORE Beef Stew Place opened can in skillet, half filled with water. Heat. Saves pan washing. Serve over split hot buttered Bisquick Biscuits.

the recipe from his mother. (The red-check label on the can was supposed to evoke her kitchen tablecloth.) But the much less romantic truth is that the stew brand was created to fill $25,000 worth of cans destined for the trash heap.

The year was 1935, and the Austin, Minnesota–based Geo. A. Hormel & Company had been canning roast beef and gravy in a government-sponsored Depression food relief program that was abruptly cut, leaving the company with half a million empty pound-and-a-half cans. Company officials decided to fill the cans with beef stew for the same hard-luck crowd, marketing it as the 15-cent "big meal in the big can."

Hormel Foods got the Dinty Moore name from a Minnesota grocery chain; it was then promptly sued by the creator of the cartoon character Dinty Moore from the comic strip *Bringing Up Father*. That conflict was settled so amicably that plaintiff George McManus ended up doing comic strip ads for the stew. And the heat-and-eat beef stew was so successful that the name was soon put on a whole line of regular Joe foods-in-a-can, including spaghetti and meatballs, corned beef and cabbage, and Irish and oxtail stews. Today Dinty Moore cans contain only beef, meatball or turkey stew, or chicken and dumplings.

But the Dinty Moore name is now also on an American Classic line of individual shelf-stable meals, including turkey and dressing, pot roast, lasagna, and (the original inspiration) roast beef and gravy; it's also on the family-sized Classic Bakes boxed meal kits that make chili and cornbread, chicken and biscuits, and (of course)

So Which Is It?

Hormel's pioneering use of micro-wavable plastic "cans" for its Dinty Moore and other products earned it a Diamond DuPont packaging award from *Packaging Digest* magazine—and a Wastemaker Award from a coalition of environmental groups concerned about excessive packaging.

George McManus's comic strip ads for Dinty Moore focused on family dinner table dilemmas rather than the corned beef and cabbage–making bar owner who shared the stew's name.

beef stew and biscuits. They're all plain, hearty, filling, and convenient, but unlike most of their latter-day competition, do not require refrigeration. This makes Dinty Moore perfect for hurricanes, food banks, camping trips, and survivalists, as well as for anyone who can't cook.

Zoom, Zoom, Zoom

In 1993 Dinty Moore sales shot up an unprecedented 23 percent following a promotion in which consumers were offered a toy Ford Explorer for 10 Dinty Moore proofs-of-purchase. The Ford Explorer was chosen because research showed that SUVs were something the brand's primary audience of lower- to lower-middle income families didn't own but very much wanted. And they weren't the only ones. In a presentation to investment analysts, Hormel president Joel Johnson attributed the Dinty Moore sales boom to a related company contest that awarded the salesman with the best Dinty Moore sales gains with a real Ford Explorer. "They're killing themselves for it," Johnson said.

Bringing Up Father comic strip stars Jiggs and Maggie make some noise for Dinty Moore in the late 1930s.

Chapter 2

POWERFUL
PACKAGES

Americans are a superficial people, foreigners who know us mainly from our movies are wont to say. But there's nothing superficial about the changes we've made to our food packaging. They've made sinful fats healthy, they've made cheese into edible art with an indefinite shelf life, and they've made soup into something that you can make in minutes rather than hours. These packages have changed expectations about how food should look, sure— but also about how it should taste and perform. When the cream whips itself, the soup is a portable powder that springs to life in an instant, and the margarine has zero calories, well, those are packaging makeover miracles that are anything but ho-hum.

Pillsbury Poppin' Fresh Dough

"Hoo-hoo, tee-hee, an actor's life for me."

The Pillsbury Doughboy, a.k.a. "Poppin' Fresh," is the literal personification of Pillsbury refrigerated dough products. He is the creation of Rudy Perz, an advertising copywriter who cracked open a can of Pillsbury Crescent Rolls one day in 1965 and, under pressure to create an advertising campaign, saw not simply dough springing forth, but a living, breathing dough boy who would both promote and help in the preparation of Pillsbury dough. To help make clear the distinction between the nonedible Doughboy character and his edible products, Perez gave him a scarf and a chef's hat, two big blue eyes, a winning smile, and Cary Grant's charm. He'd blush when a little girl kissed him, and when people gave him an affectionate poke in the stomach, he'd cut loose with a funny little giggle.

Not to Be Confused With
World War I–era American infantry-men were known as "doughboys," supposedly because doughnuts had been part of American military rations since the Civil War.

The refrigerated dough that Poppin' Fresh personifies was invented in 1930 by a Louisville, Kentucky, baker aptly named Lively Willoughby; the first few unbaked biscuits he tried storing in cardboard tubes ricocheted all around his kitchen upon opening. Lively's son got the job of scraping dough off their kitchen ceiling and floors.

Hot biscuits were a staple of Southern cooking at the time, and Willoughby was hoping to expand his local bakery business by prepar-ing biscuits that housewives only had to bake and could perhaps pass off as their own—thus beginning a great tradition of lying about the origins of Pillsbury refrigerated baked goods that continues to this day.

The approach . . .

Willoughby's experiments finally yielded a method of wrapping the dough in tinfoil and putting it in cardboard "cans" sealed with metal lids to create a pressurized package that would keep the biscuits fresh in the icebox for a week instead of a day. (Consumers sawed those early tubes open with a knife; later by aggressively whacking the tube on a countertop until the dough burst forth.) Willoughby joined forces with the Ballard & Ballard flour company of Louisville, Kentucky, and sales expanded throughout the South.

Pillsbury acquired Willoughby's 1931 refrigerated dough patent 20 years later when they purchased Ballard. Shortly after that purchase Pillsbury CEO Paul S. Gerot asked Ballard employee Lowell Armstrong and fellow Ballard OvenReady Biscuit-makers to list every single product that might be made through the refrigerated dough process. Armstrong later said, "I thought it was the craziest thing. . . . But we sat down and worked up a list of 30 to 50 products. So help me, a big share of those products are now on the market!" The Pillsbury Doughboy was the result of Pillsbury's wish to unite all their refrigerated products under a single corporate symbol.

But bringing Perz's Doughboy vision to life on the TV screen proved almost as laborious as making baked goods in pre-refrigerated dough days.

hit . . .

. . . and recovery from a 2001 Doughboy ad poking sequence.

Filling each second of Doughboy screen time took hours. The poke was accomplished with eight inter-changeable bodies with graduating degrees of belly depression. For years the Doughboy's "tee-hee" and "hoo-hoo" was supplied by Paul Frees, an actor who demonstrated his versatility by also providing the voice of the evil Boris Badenov in the *Rocky and Bullwinkle* cartoons.

A rulebook running hundreds of pages guards the Doughboy's every move. It prevented Pillsbury from getting some free publicity in a "Got Milk?" ad. (The spot was to show him mischievously washing down his cookies with the last of one family's supply of milk, but Pillsbury executives say the Dough-boy does not trick people or eat.) Pillsbury also kept the Doughboy from appearing on boxer shorts and bathroom accessories. (Could the guideline "Rear views cannot include buns" have played a roll . . . er, role?). The guide-lines did allow him to become more active post-1990, in keep-ing with Americans' growing health consciousness.

The payoff from all this careful handling: The Doughboy repeatedly wins, places, or shows in the Cartoon Q surveys of favorite food characters. In 1987 readers of *Advertising Age* magazine named him the most beloved American advertising character, above the California Raisins, Tony the Tiger, the Kool-Aid pitcher man (who had taken to the streets of Manhattan to campaign for the honor), and the (admittedly longshot) ani-mated Banner toilet paper roll.

Small wonder that, when Pillsbury was forced to sell off its baking mixes to International Multifoods as part of its 2001 takeover by General Mills, Multifoods sought joint custody of Poppin' Fresh.

Easy Cheese Aerosol (a.k.a. Snack Mate)
Behold the Power of the Aerosol Can

Jackie Kennedy brought a new energy and elegance to entertaining in America in the early 1960s—which Nabisco in 1965 exploited by introducing their Snack Mate aerosol canned cheese.

Yes, you read that right. Early ads ignored Snack Mate's obvious kinship to insecticide and toothpaste, focusing instead on the can's revolutionary decorator tip, which allowed hostesses to become artisans of cheese by creating elegant-looking canapés adorned with bright orange cheese rosettes and filigrees. Almost all were created on Nabisco crackers. If that didn't give you a clue to Nabisco's ulterior motives, the name should have. This silly string of dairy foods was created as a mate for Nabisco snack crackers just as surely as Eve was made to be a companion for Adam.

Ease and elegance took a back seat to fun in this 2002 Easy Cheese ad.

But Nabisco also wanted a cheese that was compatible with their cracker-and-cookie distribution system. So they asked the American Can Company to create a can that could be filled with hot cheese and then hermetically sealed so as not to require refrigeration. (Refrigeration can actually keep the cheese from dispensing freely.) The cans also contain nitrogen, which forces a piston at the bottom of the can upward along with some cheese when the valve is pressed. This icon of cheese art and artificiality was originally made in the heart of Wisconsin cheese country from all-natural ingredients.

By 1966 the original four flavors (American, Cheddar, Pimiento, and Swiss) were joined by the even more upscale Cheddar Blue cheese and Shrimp Cocktail. By the late 1960s, however, the nascent gourmet and natural foods movements made aerosol cheese seem pretty, well, cheesy. In 1969 Nabisco was promoting the decidedly more downscale idea of making

Snack Mate smiley-faced "Happyburgers." And nothing signaled the end of Camelot like the 1975 ad that showed a hairy hand squirting Snack Mate on an aluminum metal camping plate (thus implying that its greatest asset was shelf-stableness rather than dazzling cocktail party guests).

In 1984 Nabisco changed Snack Mate's name to Easy Cheese so people would also feel free to decorate main dishes like pizza and quiche.

Easy Cheese is now owned by Kraft and made in Springfield, Missouri, from ingredients that are more along the lines of what everyone always assumed it was.

A 1966 Snack Mate family snapshot.

Jiffy Pop Popcorn
Fun Under Foil

The 1960s were part of the clean-your-plate-there-are-starving-children-in-Africa era. Fortunately, it was also the age of Jiffy Pop, a food product that was more fun than Pop Rocks, green ketchup, and Lunchables combined.

For those born in the microwave age: Jiffy Pop is an aluminum pie plate filled with popcorn and oil and covered with a sheet of aluminum foil that grows like The Blob when you shake the pan over a hot stove by the attached wire handle. In other words it's popcorn-making at least as entertaining as its traditional movie or TV show accompaniment.

The kids' chant that ended its TV ads pretty much said it all:

"Jiffy Pop, Jiffy Pop, the magic treat
As much fun to make as it is to eat."

Popcorn was a popular theater treat for years before people began making it at home when they watched TV. But getting just the right balance of oil and kernels and heat rivals piecrust and gravy in cooking difficulty. In the '50s kitchen cupboards were filled with pots with bottoms scarred from this battle. No wonder Detroit entrepreneurs Benjamin Colman and Betty Robins thought there might be a market for a disposable pan containing proven-to-pop amounts of oil and popcorn, with a folded aluminum foil cover that kept the popcorn from flying all over the kitchen.

Their so-called E-Z Pop product went on the market in 1954 with only limited success—reportedly, a too-small aluminum foil cover caused some bottom kernels to burn. E-Z Pop employee and Robins's brother-in-law Frederick Mennen designed a spiral-wound aluminum cover to fix the problem, but Colman and other food companies turned down his innovation. So

Not Such a Jolly Time for Jiffy Pop

This fun product has unfortunately been the focus of some pretty unpleasant legal proceedings. In 1960 the corporate heir to Benjamin Colman and Betty Robins's original pop-in-pan product sued Frederick Mennen for patent infringement. Later that same year Robins filed a separate suit against Mennen, her brother-in-law. Mennen settled the latter case by agreeing to sell the Jiffy Pop company and split the assets with Robins. Jiffy Pop purchaser American Home Foods ended up having to pay on the other suit. Court documents don't say whether Jiffy Pop was served at any subsequent Mennen/Robins Thanksgiving feasts in the manner of the Indian's reconciliatory maize, but we doubt it.

Mennen brought out his newly improved Jiffy Pop pan popcorn himself.

Mennen also invented the almost-as-unique "Popcorn Tree" grocery store display racks that—together with a heavy advertising schedule—secured the product's success. Promotions featuring the magician Blackstone and the movie *Mary Poppins* highlighted the magic of a food that grew.

Sales for Jiffy Pop stayed strong until 1985—or about one minute after the popular acceptance of the microwave oven. Microwave popcorn made popcorn with cool, clean, and comparatively boring efficiency. By the time American Home Foods, the corporate inheritor of Mennen's invention, developed a microwave Jiffy Pop with an expanding see-through bag, other brands had already captured most of the market.

Sadly, although the original aluminum Jiffy Pop is still made, availability is not as good as it is for microwave popcorn; the real trick to the Jiffy Pop treat today is finding a store that can conjure you up a pan.

Pinning Down a Pop Icon

Several Internet craft sites offer instructions on how to create a decorative pin tribute to this pop (and popped) culture icon. We offer these instructions in the Frederick Mennen tradition of idea-tweaking and improvement:

1. Dunk a metal bottle cap in silver paint and allow to dry.
2. Cover a grape-sized ball of Styrofoam in glue, then roll the top in some tiny pieces of Styrofoam.
3. Glue the bottom of the ball to the inside bottom of the bottle cap.
4. Drape a small square of aluminum foil over the ball, tucking, trimming, and then gluing the ends into the side of the cap.
5. Cut an X on the top of the foil and carefully peel back to reveal Styrofoam "popcorn."
6. Fashion handle out of a paperclip or stiff wire and glue to side of bottle cap.
7. Glue a safety pin to the bottom of the cap.

Pringles Potato Chips
A New Use for Tennis Ball Cans

IT'S OUT OF THE BAG!
Unbroken potato chips that stay fresh!

Enough of that squashy misfit bag! Pringle's Newfangled Potato Chips come in their own crushproof, airtight canister so they're always fresh and unbroken, even after they're open! And they're perfectly shaped so they stack together...deliciously big, unbroken and beautiful! Just pour out a bowlful and chomp into the most tantalizing taste in the whole crunchy world!

This first Pringles print ad (from 1968) had a lot of explaining to do.

Procter & Gamble engineers usually spend their time formulating cleaners that will remove stains or designing diapers that won't leak. But in 1961, the company asked their engineers to answer consumers' complaints that potato chips were too greasy, broke too easily, and got stale too quickly. The intrepid crew set out to make the perfect potato chip.

The culmination of P&G's research and development (which didn't reach full national distribution until 1975) were chips made by combining dried potato flakes with flour and water to form a dough that could be cut out into a perfectly uniform shape, cooked in curved molds, and then stacked in sturdy "tennis ball" cans. They named the chips after Pringles Street in Finneytown, Ohio, near Procter & Gamble's Cincinnati headquarters, in part because of the word's alliterative kinship with potato chips and Procter & Gamble.

After an initial spurt of curiosity buying, sales of the prom-

Future Food
Before he became America's finest science fiction writer (if not, as one *Washington Post* writer has said, America's greatest living writer, period), Gene Wolfe helped design the machines that make one of America's most famous futuristic snack foods.

Canned Potato Chip Crisis

The arrival of Pringles and other, similar fabricated potato chips in the late 1960s scared the bejesus out of "traditional" potato chip makers—so much so that their trade organization went to court to stop these dried potato imposters from trading under the potato chip's good name. After losing the court case, the Potato Chip Institute turned to the FDA, which took two years to say that in two years these new chips would have to clearly state that they were made from dried potatoes. By then, sales of Pringles and the other prefab chips were so small that nobody cared.

ising Pringles dropped precipitously. Perhaps P&G had taken consumer demands too seriously: Like the Stepford Wives' husbands, potato chip eaters decided perfection wasn't what they wanted after all (especially if it meant a chip with the texture of tennis-can cardboard).

The long development and testing time also worked against

Single-serve Pringles debuted in 2002.

the brand. The engineers started their work on Pringles when products of American technology were all the rage, but by the time they had finished, homey, hippie values (and foods) were in. P&G tried to bridge the generation gap by creating an old-fashioned gay 1890s gentleman logo for their "newfangled" potato chips. But Pringles never really met the company's sales expectations. For almost 20 years, Pringles topped lists of famous food flops. In business story after business story, investment analysts wondered aloud why P&G didn't let this cold potato drop.

In 1992, having yet to sell enough to fully max out the production capacity of its single Pringles plant in Tennessee, someone in Procter's foreign division suggested making a few more cans and shipping them to Europe—thus marking the beginning of Pringles' rebirth as a global food phenomenon. By 1999 Pringles were being sold in 40 countries, and sales had increased from $130 million to $1 billion. So much for the idea that Europeans have more refined taste.

1967   1979   1983

Or maybe not. Even P&G admits that its foreign success is largely due to technical issues, including the ease with which retailers can stack up the cans and Pringles' 15-month shelf life (due to the product's low moisture content and oxygen-reducing, gas-flush packaging—Pringles contain no preservatives). P&G also caters to foreign tastes with export Pringles flavors like crispy curry, mild consommé, and usushio.

Pringles sales have also been on the upswing in the U.S. since the early '90s, thanks to American workaholic lifestyles that prize foods that will not crush in a briefcase; the chips can also be pulled out of the back of a desk drawer months after purchase and still be as fresh as the day they were mass-produced. In fact, nerds at Netscape meet in a conference room named after their favorite high-tech potato snack. And the saddle-shaped roof of the Sydney Olympic Stadium was inspired by the potato crisp engineers were eating while they were designing it.

Multipack "Snack Stacks" in futuristic flying formation.

1989   1992   1996

Beam Me Up, Mr. Pringles

Pringles may be handy for snacking, but their empty cans are also popular for hacking. That's because the Pringles can makes a great signal booster for people trying to log on to wireless computer networks. The Secret Service has even used them to probe security holes in government computer systems.

The Pringles can's long tube shape enables it to be pointed at specific buildings, and its aluminum inner lining acts like a satellite dish, collecting signals and sending them to a laptop's wireless card. Best of all, the Pringles antenna can be constructed for less than $10 with instructions from the Internet.

I Can't Believe It's Not Butter! Spray
We Can't Believe They Dumped Fabio

The Pump-O-Meter

A five-pump serving of I Can't Believe It's Not Butter! Spray is almost like eating nothing. That's because of government food labeling rules that allow manufacturers to round fractions down to zero. Keep pumping and this stuff will begin to have the consequences of real food. Here's a guide to the damage that can be done at higher levels of pumping.

12 pumps:
 10 calories, 1 gram of fat
25 pumps:
 20 calories, 2 grams of fat
37 pumps:
 30 calories, 3 grams of fat
50 pumps:
 40 calories, 4 grams of fat
 And so on, up to about 1,130 pumps or sprays, when the bottle will be done and you should have some killer first-finger muscles from all the pumping.

I Can't Believe It's Not Butter! Spray dispenses a butter substitute out of a Windex bottle. If that doesn't make you lose your appetite, seeing the way the oily yellow goblets land on your baked potato will. Frankly? It looks like a dog mistook the spud for a fire hydrant.

And yet this product has legions of devoted fans, including those nutty nutritionists at the Washington, D.C.–based Center for Science in the Public Interest (and like Mikey, they hate everything).

Why? I Can't Believe It's Not Butter! Spray contains zero calories, zero fat, zero cholesterol, and doesn't taste half bad. In other words it's a dieter's vision of heaven.

The regular stick version of I Can't Believe It's Not Butter! was invented by the J.H. Filbert Company in 1979. The company already made a margarine named after J.H. Filbert's wife: Mrs. Filbert's. "I Can't Believe It's Not Butter!" was supposedly this same woman's spontaneous reaction to first trying what was then America's only bread spread flavored with cholesterol-free buttermilk. In the interest of pleasing the boss and brainwashing the public, the full sentence became its official name. In 1995, I Can't Believe It's Not Butter! also became the first spread or margarine offered in spray form. The spray consists of small amounts of soybean oil, buttermilk, and salt suspended in a large amount of nutritionally benign water (which explains its sinlessness).

Advertising for I Can't Believe It's Not Butter! (hereafter to be referred to as ICBINB, lest it take as long to read this entry as to churn butter) made light of America's romance with butter, showing unknown actors playing lovers in a train station or on a ballroom dance floor and alluding to a secret love: "a love of butter . . . spoiled by cholesterol."

To launch ICBINB Spray, however, the company recruited Fabio, the heartthrob with a margarine-colored mane and similarly self-aggrandizing name. The plots for his ads were ripped right out of the romance novels Fabio's image adorns—ripped out and then generously slathered with butter substitute. In one ad, a sculptress chisels on a statue of Adonis and moans, "Oh darling, I wish you were really here." Suddenly, the muscle-studded Fabio emerges from the crumbling marble—not to seize the pining maiden, but to munch a spread-smeared muffin and cry, "I Can't Believe It's Not Butter!"

ICBINB executives called the Fabio hire a goof. But the joke was lost on members of the Fabio International Fan Club who deconstructed each ad on an Internet forum. (Typical was one January 2000 member complaint about

Just when you thought your fantasy was out of reach... we put it at your fingertips.

A few Fabio-lous ICBINB ads and promotions from the mid- to late 1990s.

Pumping Her Man for a Diamond Bracelet

One of the many contest promotions ICBINB devised when Fabio was spokesman encouraged entrants to write an essay comparing their significant other's romantic qualities to the super hunk-man. Here's an excerpt from an entry by Dawn Nichols of Jordan, Minnesota, which earned her a two-carat diamond bracelet and lots of publicity.

I can't believe it's not Fabio! He's so masculine and sturdy, yet gentle and soft. . . . He loves to butter me up with sweetness, and then revels as I melt all over him like he is fresh-baked bread. . . . He prepares a feast of kisses, caresses and soft words, all sautéed in love served on a platter of commitment. I am eager to go to his table and partake. Like butter to my lips, the richness of taste lingers in my heart. . . .

One question: If Nichols's husband is so romantic, why did she have to enter a contest to get a diamond bracelet? Fifteen hundred dollars would seem a small price to pay to avoid the ribbing he must have endured after word of this essay spread.

ICBINB Semiotics

I Can't Believe It's Not Butter! is a mouthful to most and a puzzle to some.

The name implies ICBINB is not butter, but doesn't completely rule out the possibility that it *is* butter. That smidgen of doubt—or possible deception—fueled the English butter lobby's successful bid to block Unilever from advertising ICBINB on TV in Great Britain in the early '90s.

Members of the now defunct ICBINB Internet newsgroup spent years and hundreds of megabytes trying to understand the use of "It" as it appears in the product name. Many argued that "I Can't Believe This Isn't Butter!" would have been a much better name.

This confusion has not stopped other food companies from creating names that double as sales pitches. These include Just 2 Good! and Light Done Right salad dressings, and Green Giant Gimmie Gimmie Garlic Chicken Pasta frozen meal kit. Can babies named I Can't Believe I'm So Smart! and Ain't She Sweet? be far behind?

a new Sleeping Beauty–themed Fabio commercial in which he appears hardly at all and, even worse, as a lowly wagon driver.)

The brand also sponsored many contests and at least one premium, a book called *I Can't Believe It's Not Butter! A Guide to Food & Romance*—although the food tips and romantic pointers did not intersect, which is probably for the best. (We've heard of massage oil, but spraying your sweetheart with oleo is like making love with a raincoat on.)

That could be why the brand finally dropped the hunky Fabio in 2001 in favor of a tamer—though no less wacky— marketing approach. On Mother's Day 2002, for instance, the company set up 50 beds in New York's Grand Central Station so that 50 mothers could be serenaded by the squeaky clean Donny Osmond while eating breakfast breads topped with plenty of you-know-what.

The I Can't Believe It's Not Butter! product line, circa 1997.

Reddi-wip
"Glamour Desserts at the Touch of a Finger"

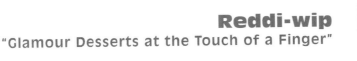

Serve this dessert masterpiece tonight...
Frozen Berries'n Reddi-wip

Make it in minutes with Bisquick and fresh, real cream Reddi-wip

This mid-'50s ad focused on the artistic possibilities of Reddi-wip's decorator tip.

Today aerosol spray cans dispense everything from furniture polish to deodorant to vegetable oil. In the early 1940s, though, aerosols were used almost exclusively for insecticide. It took a truly unusual person with an equally unusual name—Aaron S. "Bunny" Lapin (as in French for rabbit)—to envision dispensing whipped cream out of such a container.

Lapin was a law school dropout who happened by his brother-in-law's Chicago dairy company one day in 1941 while a salesman for Sta-Wip, a fake whipped cream product, was making his pitch. At a time when wartime restrictions made it impossible to make real whipped cream, Lapin and his brother-in-law, Mark Lipsky, thought there might be a market for a substitute. So Lipsky bought the Sta-Wip company and gave it to Lapin to run. Within two weeks Lapin was making money. He sold the fake

Dutch Treat
Reddi-wip is made in only one place in the United States: Holland, Michigan, where it plays second fiddle only to the town's famed tulip displays. Let's hope they have reliable backup generators.

The first cans of Reddi-wip had hardly hit supermarket shelves before Bunny Lapin was dreaming of other uses for the aerosol valves his company had created. As early as 1951 he playfully squirted shaving cream on a newspaper reporter, although he ultimately decided to simply sell his valves to shaving product powerhouses Schick and Barbasol.

The aerosol ideas Lapin did pursue—an aerosol milk shake called Touch 'N Shake, an aerosol malted milk called Touch 'N Malt, a cinnamon-flavored margarine called Touch 'N Spred, and an aerosol cleaner called Touch 'N Clean—were all flops. The cleaner was just ahead of its time.

Lapin's other winning idea was for aerosol-dispensed foam insulating products. Lapin died in 1999, but his St. Louis–based Clayton Corporation, now run by his son Byron, still sells aerosol valves and the Touch 'N Foam (below) and Touch 'N Seal canned insulation.

whipped cream to soda fountains along with a reusable dispensing gun. When fountain owners complained that the product sometimes spoiled before they were able to use it all up, Lapin created smaller, disposable guns.

Next Lapin camped out in the office of a Philadelphia aerosol can company until its owner agreed to sell him cans on credit. By this time University of Illinois chemist Charles Goetz had already discovered that milk released from a vessel pressurized with nitrous oxide would foam. Lapin got a cousin to build on Goetz's work by designing a dispensing valve that kept the gas that whipped the cream inside the can. Then, in 1947, he began reselling the cans, the valves, and the right to make the newly named *real* whipped cream Reddi-wip to dairies around the country. (Wartime cream restrictions were by now lifted.) By 1951 he had outfitted most of his extended family with Cadillacs and was living in Gloria Swanson's old Hollywood mansion.

"Hurrah for Reddi-wip!" Say Millions of Holiday Hostesses

In the mid-'50s Reddi-wip was advertised as "the way to create holiday excitement for . . . all the gay home events of the season."

Reddi-wip teamed up with Bisquick in a series of ads in the late 1950s.

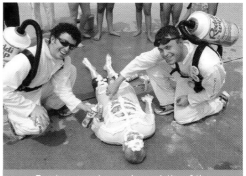

Two improv actors and one victim of the Reddi-wip-style fun they brought to summer festivals across the U.S. in 2002.

Whipping Up Interest in Aerosol Food

Bunny Lapin was lounging by a pool in Hollywood one day when a ping-pong ball fell in his lap. He struck up a conversation with its owner—the wife of radio star Arthur Godfrey—and soon life-sized cardboard cut-outs of Godfrey holding a Reddi-wip can were in supermarkets across the country. In accompanying print ads, a chef's toque–topped Godfrey called Reddi-wip "Magic! At the merest touch of your finger, out swirls fresh, rich cream, whipped automatically."

"No work, no fuss, no muss. No bowl and beater to wash," said another ad that called Reddi-wip a "dessert miracle." "Reddi-wip is economical too . . . see how it transforms even the thriftiest budget dessert into an exciting creation that's fit for a king."

Other ads addressed to mothers stressed the nutritional benefits of Reddi-wip's real dairy ingredients. One even went so far as to suggest luring "cereal rebels" to breakfast by topping their corn flakes with Reddi-wip: "See how eagerly he eats it without coaxing. For Reddi-wip adds a party-touch at breakfast— makes any cereal seem as gay as a French confection!"

Reddi-wip is still made from real milk and cream. This surprises many people but apparently interests few, even in this era of pure and natural foods. People surveyed by the company in the mid-'80s were much more interested in the can—the sound it makes, the way it decorates, and its unique red-and-white label. In the mid- to late 1990s, the company responded with an ad campaign that made Reddi-wip the Absolut vodka of the dairy case. The award-winning print ad campaign decorated the can in Christmas lights, dressed it up like a pilgrim, and conjured it out of ice cream, a cow, even a semi.

PAM
Guilt-Free Grease in a Can

Nobody ever really says, "Hey, let's have some Pam!" Not even the newfangled garlic- and butter-flavored Pams, which are actually intended to be sprayed onto foods rather than pots and pans.

Pam is instead more of a food *enabler*. Its oil is suspended in a solution with lecithin and sprayed in a way that enables it to fry food or grease pans using a fraction of the fat and calories of butter, margarine, or other oils. That's what earned Pam the number 2 spot on *Cooking Light* magazine's list of top 10 healthy foods of the twentieth century (below only boneless, skinless chicken breasts).

Grateful dieters everywhere can lay all the pounds Pam has saved them at the grave of Arthur E. Meyerhoff. Meyerhoff was a successful Chicago ad executive (Wrigley's Chewing Gum was a client) in search of a side business in the mid-1950s when he put an ad in the *Wall Street Journal* asking for new product ideas. Among the respondents were two chemists who had developed a Pam-like oil-in-suspension; what they lacked was a convenient delivery system. Meyerhoff bought their idea; then, with the help of business partner Leon Rubin and

Can you keep your lasagna from sticking? Yes you can with

A PRODUCT OF ConAgra Foods®

A 2003 Pam print ad.

An early PAM "celebrity" endorser.

several hired scientists, he tweaked their formula so that it could be neatly and conveniently sprayed.

The next problem was getting grocers to put Pam in the baking aisle rather than in the aerosol section, which at that time consisted of not-exactly-appetizing insecticides and hair spray. He also had to convince consumers that the stuff was not poisonous like the insecticides, and was in fact safe to spray on their cooking pans, recalls his daughter, Judith Meyerhoff Yale.

To develop consumer trust, Meyerhoff systematically approached the best-known cooking personalities in every city where they were introducing Pam. He would ask them to star in ads in that market. "Some of them were crotchety, but that didn't matter because it was their credibility he was after," Yale says.

These unconventional ads and supermarkets' willingness to properly shelve Pam succeeded beyond Meyerhoff's wildest dreams. Financially speaking, Pam ended up being more successful than Meyerhoff's ad agency. It was an even bigger success for Boyle-Midway, the company Meyerhoff sold it to in 1971.

What was the key to Pam's success? In part it was the healthy eating trends that Pam met so naturally. In part it's because Pam outgrew its original kitchen aims to become a household staple that consumers use to do everything from quieting squeaks, to preventing snow from sticking to plastic shovels, to making their muscles shine in bodybuilding competitions, to getting burrs out of a dog's coat, to loosening a stuck ring. In other words, in its versatility, Pam is like edible WD-40.

Pam was originally called Pam Dry Fry.

Unauthorized Use

Schoolboy football descended to a new level of sliminess in 2001 when two different football teams sprayed themselves with Pam so they'd be harder to tackle.

The Loveland High School football team in Colorado slid to victory in their '01 match with rival Greely Central (though they were banned from participating in the playoffs). But Sacramento State lost their Pam-powered November '02 game. These scholar-athletes (and we use the term very loosely) apparently hadn't realized that having Pam on their hands would also—hello!—make it hard for them to hold onto the ball.

Lipton Cup-a-Soup
"Quickalicious!"

Al Carlson remembers the day Lipton food scientist Pete Andrews offhandedly suggested that he might be able to make soup faster than the 10- to 12-minute cooking time required for the dried Lipton Soup Mixes Carlson was then managing. At a time when fast food was the order of the day, this was like someone offhandedly mentioning they had just won the lottery.

"I went crazy," Carlson recalled. "I said, 'Are you kidding? Let's do it!'"

Andrews and others in the lab had apparently been working on the technology for some time, because it was only a matter of days before Andrews had brewed him up a cup of soup simply by adding boiling water to a powder. The key to the invention of the world's first instant soup was the invention of precooked noodles. The soup also contained spices, dehydrated vegetables, and, in some cases, meat pieces that were dried and preserved with a proprietary technology that won Lipton an Industrial Achievement Award from *Food Technology* magazine. Several months later Carlson was invited on a tour of the plant where Cup-a-Soup was being stockpiled in anticipation of the 1970 launch. Initial flavors included tomato, onion, pea, spring vegetable, and chicken noodle.

He arrived to find "warehouses the size of aircraft carriers filled with the stuff," which made him break out in a sweat and sent him running back to his office to figure out how he was going to sell it all.

Lipton's first effort to win over consumers was a series of ads that suggested eating Cup-a-Soup for lunch, mid-morning, mid-afternoon—even as a bedtime snack. (That last idea was advertised with sultry jazz trumpet music accompaniment.)

Carlson, Diller, and their PR tour "handler."

Whenever you chose to eat it, Cup-a-Soup was "Quickalicious."

Carlson demonstrated the product to radio DJs and later enlisted the help of comedienne Phyllis Diller, who whipped up batches for various TV talk show hosts. "She would be joking with Mike Douglas and then all of a sudden ask if he'd like a nice cup of soup," said Carlson, who accompanied the unofficial spokeswoman on her talk show rounds. The important thing was that people were getting to see a food that used to take their grandmothers all day to prepare, made in an instant. First-year sales were an astonishing $36.5 million.

These days Carlson attributes the product's success as much to its individuality as its technology. "Lifestyles had changed so people were no longer sitting down at the table together anymore. The individual packets fit right in with that."

Cup-a-Soup pretty much owned the instant soup market in America until the late 1980s, when ramen noodle soups began to offer serious competition. These soups contained lots more noodles than Cup-a-Soup and could be conveniently prepared in their own cardboard containers. Campbell's joined the fray in the late 1990s with liquid soups in individual microwavable cups. As retro as dehydrated vegetables and freeze-dried meat might seem today, Cup-a-Soup still contains a lot less fat than ramen (which is fried) and won't weigh down backpacks and briefcases the way Campbell's products do.

Cup-a-Soup Chicken

Is It Kentucky Fried Chicken Yet?

Lipton Cup-a-Soup's whole raison d'être is that it doesn't require any cooking. But it is sometimes (perversely?) used in cooking, as in this Internet recipe for a Shake 'n Bake–like chicken coating.

1 package Lipton Tomato Cup-a-Soup instant soup mix
3 tablespoons each packed brown sugar and dry parsley
2 tablespoons each garlic salt, onion salt, thyme, and instant chicken bouillon
1 tablespoon each rosemary, oregano, ground sage, and paprika
1 teaspoon each pepper and marjoram
1 1/2 cups flour
1 cup milk
8 chicken pieces

Combine all ingredients through marjoram and pulverize in a blender or rub through a fine strainer. Mix 5 to 6 tablespoons of mixture with the flour. Moisten chicken pieces with milk and roll in flour coating. Fry until golden brown or bake at 350°F for 45 to 60 minutes. Store leftover seasoning mix in an airtight container. Serves 4 to 6.

Chapter 3

TRIUMPHS OF TECHNOLOGY

Food in its natural state spoils, typically takes work to get into an edible form, and varies in quality. But the foods in this chapter are not bound by these unappealing conventions. They represent the triumph of technology over food's natural imperfections. While it may not be nice to fool Mother Nature, it sure makes eating a lot quicker and easier, not to mention more predictable.

Coffee-mate Non-Dairy Creamer
The Un-Cream

NEW! A NON-DAIRY COFFEE CREAMER...COFFEE-MATE!
Brings out the true flavor of coffee. Never hides it. Costs less than 1¢ a serving. Needs no refrigeration. Blends instantly!

Look for new Coffee-mate at your Exchange or Commissary. Made by Carnation

Coffee-mate flows freely, never cakes in the jar

A 1963 ad extolling Coffee-mate's virtues to the military crowd.

People today want everything to be all natural. But all-natural foods rarely offer consistent quality. And all-natural foods preserved or put into new forms often don't look or taste as good as fake.

Instant powdered coffee creamer is the perfect example. The first powdered creamer to hit supermarkets, in 1952, was called Pream. It was made of dehydrated cream, milk sugar, and nonfat milk solids. In other words, it was the real deal. But the processing required to dry it made it taste terrible. And the proteins in the milk made the product spill out in unsightly clumps.

Carnation food scientists were asked to come up with something better six years later, and they soon identified the problem: the real milk and cream. The product tasted better when the butterfat was replaced with vegetable oil, and the clumping was virtually eliminated if most of the milk protein was dumped as well. Carnation's introductory ads trumpeted new Coffee-mate Non-Dairy Creamer as an "amazing discovery" that

Unauthorized Uses

Coffee creamer has been used to whiten clothes (when mixed with water to create a soaking solution), clean dry erase boards, defoam fish tanks, and simulate snow and sandstorms on TV weather forecasts. Mixed with two parts hot water and chilled, Coffee-mate powder can also serve as a general substitute for milk or cream.

"eliminates the stale cooked taste of old-fashioned powdered creamers," costs less than milk, flows freely, and "keeps sweet and fresh indefinitely without refrigeration."

What more could anyone ask for in a creamer? Nothing, which is why Coffee-mate became and remained the leading powdered coffee creamer in America, capturing nearly half of all sales for almost 30 years with virtually no change (not even in the amber-colored screw-top jar).

With the slowdown in coffee consumption in the late 1980s, however, Coffee-mate executives began acting with the freneticism of people high on caffeine. New Lite Coffee-mate was followed in quick succession by liquid and fat free. The liquid performed similarly to the powder but lasted only about a week after opening instead of indefinitely. It also was more expensive and had more calories and fat than milk or rehydrated Coffee-mate powder. Nevertheless, liquid nondairy creamers have been a big success, rising from only 4 percent of the nondairy creamer market in 1990 to 21 percent today—most food industry analysts believe because they seem more like real milk and cream.

In the second half of the 1990s, the company introduced a dizzying variety of flavored creamers in hopes of capturing the new market of flavored gourmet coffee fans. At the turn of the twenty-first century, all the Coffee-mate products got a packaging facelift. The new curvy plastic bottles appeared to be copying the containers for the caffeine-enhanced energy drinks favored by Generation X and Y drinkers.

It's too early to say if the new packages have created any Coffee-mate converts, but they have been enthusiastically embraced by crafters, who have already posted instructions on the Internet for making them into Christmas Santas and toy bowling pins.

Cool Whip
A Dream of a Cream

Whipped cream that comes already whipped, keeps for weeks, and is cheaper and has fewer calories than the real thing: Even the housewives who suggested this miracle food to General Foods marketers as part of a 1965 survey must have thought it sounded like a dream—along with kids who run home from school to do their homework and husbands who always put the dirty dishes in the dishwasher.

Imagine their surprise when, in less than two years, a collection of emulsifers, stabilizers, oils, and sugars meeting all their requirements debuted in supermarkets in Seattle, Washington, and Syracuse, New York. It was called Cool Whip mainly because the words *wonder* and *miracle* and *dream* were already taken by a bread, a salad dressing, and a dry whipped topping mix that were actually much less miraculous.

Cool Whip is new...but the taste is pure old-fashioned.

Luscious-looking desserts lent their appeal to this 1967 introductory ad for Cool Whip.

You know the rule about never refreezing defrosted food? Well, when it comes to Cool Whip, you can forget it. Cool Whip's shelf life can be extended significantly by multiple thawings and refreezing. It's just one of many ways in which Cool

You've Come a Long Way Baby—Not

We probably have Martha Stewart to blame for the popularity of the link on the Cool Whip Web site that offers instructions on how to make "the perfect dollop": Draw a spoon across the surface of a Cool Whip container to create "waves," scoop a few of them up with a spoon, and then carefully transfer them to the surface of a piece of pie or dish of pudding (assuming you have nothing better to do with your time).

Better Than Sex Cake

1 18.5-ounce box German chocolate cake mix
1 14-ounce can sweetened condensed milk
2 cups hot fudge, caramel, or butterscotch ice cream topping
4 Heath candy bars, crushed
1 12-ounce container Cool Whip, thawed

Bake the cake as per package directions. While cake is still warm, use the non-business end of a wooden spoon to poke holes in it. Pour the condensed milk over the cake and let cool. Pour ice cream topping over the cake and let sit in refrigerator for 30 minutes. Sprinkle with crushed Heath bars, then frost with Cool Whip. Store leftovers in refrigerator. Serves 10–12.

Whip hardly acts like a food. Fat-free Cool Whip Free is even more amazing when you consider that one of regular Cool Whip's main ingredients is oil.

But whipped cream should be homemade—not high tech. While ads for General Foods' sister product Tang played up its technological gee-whizness, the Cool Whip ads played it down. "Cool Whip is new . . . but the taste is pure old-fashioned," read an introductory ad that showed it topping such traditional desserts as pie, pudding, Jell-O, and strawberry shortcake.

Soon Cool Whip was starring in recipes alongside an extraordinary number of other General Foods products. (The prize, if there was one, probably went to the test kitchen employee who invented Glorified Rice, containing Cool Whip, Jell-O, and Minute Rice.) Cool Whip was also the mortar in a whole array of quickie gourmet dessert recipes all the rage in the late 1960s and early 1970s, including mousse (Cool Whip whipped into instant pudding); chiffon pie (Cool Whip whipped into unset Jell-O); and trifle (Cool Whip layered with pound cake, Jell-O Pudding, and Birds Eye frozen strawberries—or only one fewer General Foods product than what's called for in Glorified Rice). Rare is the community or church cookbook even today that does not call for Cool Whip in at least one recipe (and usually many more).

Cool Whip Lite (introduced in 1990) and Cool Whip Free (in 1996) have achieved rock-star status with dieters who pour them on low-appeal fruit desserts and anemic "diet" ice cream or combine them with angel food cake, Sugar Free Jell-O, Light Philadelphia Cream Cheese, and reduced-fat peanut butter in "lightened-up" recipes for traditionally high-calorie pies and cakes.

This is not even to mention the ubiquitous reusable plastic Cool Whip tub. It's safe to say that millions of Cool Whip sales have been prompted by the disappointment of opening one of those white containers only to find leftover green beans.

Sweet 'N Low
The First, the Worst, the Favorite

Sweet 'N Low is the most artificial-tasting artificial sweetener on the market. And yet Sweet 'N Low sells more boxes than any of its rivals. Those little pink packets also grace virtually every restaurant table in the country.

Early boxes and ads featured the silhouette of a svelte Sweet 'N Low user. She was later replaced by photos of coffee and cereal being sweetened with the stuff.

No, Americans are not masochists. We're cheapskates. Sweet 'N Low is two to four times cheaper than its better-tasting baby blue rival, Equal. As America's oldest artificial sweetener, Sweet 'N Low has a taste people can't shake as easily as they can the packets.

Sweet 'N Low's success could also be the result of the special brand of simpatico between the perennial dieters who buy it and the saga of its Sisyphean creator, Benjamin Eisenstadt.

Eisenstadt's first business was a cafeteria and bar located across the street from a naval shipyard in Brooklyn. Business boomed until World War II ended and most of his customers went home. Eisenstadt's second venture, a bagged-tea business, was headed in the same downward direction in 1945 when Eisenstadt's wife, Betty, had a brainstorm. Remembering the mess their former customers had made of the cafeteria's open sugar bowls, Betty suggested that the tea-bagging machines might be used to bag small packets of sugar. Eisenstadt brought her brilliant idea to a sugar company

Most Famous Sweet 'N Low Dirty Joke
Q: What's the difference between sugar and Sweet 'N Low?
A: Sugar's when you kiss someone on the lips.

Unauthorized Use

🚫 Women coloring their hair at home can rinse with a Sweet 'N Low-and-water solution to reduce irritation.

Why Sweet 'N Low Does Not Equal Equal

In the early 1980s, the Searle company approached Benjamin Eisenstadt's son, Marvin, about launching their new NutraSweet sweetener under the Sweet 'N Low brand name. But in a business decision some say rivaled his father's long-ago meeting with a sugar company executive, Eisenstadt said no. So Searle went with the name Equal, and the Eisenstadt family's Cumberland Packing Corp. expanded its product line to include fake salt, fake butter, and later, a NutraSweet rip-off called NatraTaste (but as of yet, no more Instant Life Sea-Monkeys).

executive—who promptly ripped it off.

After receiving what had to have been a wicked tongue-lashing from Betty, Eisenstadt went on to make the country's first takeout packets of soy sauce, ketchup, and even Sea-Monkeys before he came up with the idea of artificial sweetener packets. Soon the Eisenstadts' son, Marvin, who had studied chemistry at the University of Vermont, had figured out how to mix saccharin with dextrose and other ingredients to make a granulated low-calorie sugar substitute.

It was 1957, a time when artificial sweeteners were mainly used by diabetics and were available only in liquid or pill form. The Eisenstadts' pink packets turned the medicine into a food. The unique pink color distinguished them from sugar and presumably appealed to the fairer sex who powered the '60s dieting craze, thereby forever sealing Sweet 'N Low's sweet success.

A tin replica of the original Sweet 'N Low box created for the sweetener's 40th anniversary in 1997.

Sweet 'N Low packets custom made for the White House and boxer Sugar Ray Robinson.

The Part of This Book That Justifies My Expensive English Literature Degree

Sweet 'N Low's name and musical staff logo were inspired by a song that was itself inspired by a Tennyson poem. In 1863 Joseph Barnby wrote music to this section of Tennyson's "The Princess," a poem about a princess who forswears men but eventually falls for one. (No MP3 of this song is currently available.)

Sweet and low, sweet and low,
Wind of the western sea,
Low, low, breathe and blow,
Wind of the western sea!
Over the rolling waters go,
Come from the dying moon, and blow,
Blow him again to me;
While my little one,
*   while my pretty one, sleeps.*

Tang
OJ for Astronauts

Tang rocketed to success with the U.S. space program and fell off most folks' radar screens about five minutes after Neil Armstrong walked on the moon. This was right about when the space program itself began to lose its grip on the public's imagination.

Contrary to popular belief, however, Tang was not invented for the astronauts. In fact, General Foods scientists had the idea to create an instant breakfast drink companion to instant coffee in 1955, or three years before the

This morning, he will drink Tang.

And then drive his lunar roving vehicle out towards the half-light of the limits of Earthshine.
This will happen. This year, man will actually drive an automotive vehicle on the moon.
And Tang will be close by. The same instant breakfast drink that's on your kitchen table. Orange-flavored Tang with more vitamin C than orange juice.
Nutritious Tang.

For breakfast tomorrow.

This 1971 ad told of Tang's role in man's first motorized exploration of the moon.

first monkey rode into space. They wanted a powder with all the vitamin C and A of orange juice that would not spoil or cake, and that could be mixed with water in an instant. In other words, they wanted to best Mother Nature.

It took two years to assemble the right combination of chemicals, all of which happened to be white. They included sugar, citric acid (to provide tartness), gum arabic, sodium carboxymethylcellulose, calcium phosphate (to prevent caking),

Cola Star Wars
Astronauts still do drink Tang in space. In fact, in the mid-'80s, *Challenger* astronauts took the fizz out of Pepsi and Coke's $14.25-million race to put soft drinks into space with the frank admission that they preferred Tang. The facts that the shuttle had no refrigerator to chill the soft drinks and that Tang can be made with cold water from the space plane's cooling system could have had something to do with that preference.

NEW TROPICAL TREMOR

INCREASES LUNCHTIME TRADING POWER BY 300%

Tang

Tang's orangoutang spokesman introduced a new ready-to-drink flavor in 2000.

sodium citrate, vitamin C, hydrogenated vegetable oil, vitamin A, and BHA (a preservative). Consumer tests ate up another two years. They steered General Foods marketers to the orange color, which in turn led to the tangerine-y name.

Tang's long development process was costly. But like the annoying traffic jam that ultimately prevents you from being in the bank for the fatal robbery, it had the benefit of delaying Tang's national launch until the U.S. space program was under way. Indeed, Tang's marketing campaign splashed down from heaven one day in 1965 with a phone call from NASA saying they thought Tang would be the perfect space food. General Foods hopped aboard with ad simulations of actor-astronauts drinking Tang in space (filmed with fuzzy lenses to simulate the crude space transmissions) and rode it to spectacular sales.

Moms felt good about Tang's vitamins. They also felt good about participating in what they thought would be only one of the first "small steps" toward a future of highly engineered foods that would free them forever from cares about nutrition, cooking, and food spoilage.

Or at least that's what they thought before the course correction of the natural and gourmet food movements of the 1970s, and the not unrelated waning interest in outer-space science, both of which were bad for Tang. One consequence was the addition of the first real orange juice solids to Tang. Another was not one but two *Saturday Night Live* skits mocking Tang: Jane Curtain and Gilda Radner's Loopner ladies drank it by the gallon; Dan Akroyd's Beldar Conehead preferred to eat it dry.

In the time-pressed '80s and '90s, mixing Tang just seemed like too much work. After several years of sales losses, Tang management reconstituted the brand with ready-to-drink Tang in several nervous-sounding flavors (Fruit Frenzy, Berry Panic, and Orange Uproar) and a new pun-based campaign starring an "orangoutang" (hey, it worked for Hawaiian Punch). But echoes of Tang's space-age origins remain—in the brand's simian star and suck-from-a-straw packaging.

Unauthorized Uses

The citric acid in Tang makes it useful for everything from shampooing greasy hair, to cleaning toilet bowls and dishwashers, to zapping warts (dab a Tang-and-water paste on the wart and cover with a Band-Aid), according to author Joey Green and visitors to his www.wackyuses.com Web site.

Sanka
Sleepytime Coffee

"I drink all the coffee I want...

I get all the sleep I need!"

DON'T STOP DRINKING COFFEE...
JUST STOP DRINKING CAFFEIN!

DELICIOUS IN
EITHER INSTANT OR
REGULAR FORM

Products of General Foods

NEW EXTRA-RICH
SANKA COFFEE
It's delicious! It's 97% caffein-free!
It lets you sleep!

A 1952 ad showing how busy working gals could drink fuel tank–sized pots of Sanka coffee without losing out on their beauty sleep.

Some drink coffee for its caffeine kick; others for its rich, bold, bracing, mountain-grown, Juan Valdez–picked, aromatic flavor. Sanka doesn't have any of those things. And yet it's survived—and at times thrived—on supermarket shelves for more than 80 years.

For almost half that time, Sanka was synonymous with decaffeinated coffee. In fact, prior to 1980, it was the word used for decaffeinated coffee on most restaurant menus. Order it in those days and a little tray with a small carafe of hot water and the trademark Halloween-orange packet would appear. This little Sanka tea ceremony made some people feel special; others, like unpaid kitchen help. *New York Times* columnist Marion Burros was among those who complained about having to make her own coffee in restaurants that bothered to mold their butter into flowers.

He Didn't Get His Jolt from Caffeine
One of the most shocking revelations from lawyer Morris Engelberg's tell-all book about Joe DiMaggio was that the baseball-great-turned-Mr.-Coffee-huckster mostly drank instant Sanka.

Sanka's heyday was the health-crazed 1960s and '70s. Whereas health in America used to mean treating disease and injuries, suddenly it meant overall wellness and a healthy lifestyle—which very well might mean cutting back on caffeine.

In a series of Sanka ads running from 1977 to 1982, actor Robert Young traded on his starring roles on both *Father Knows Best* and *Marcus Welby, M.D.* to talk about the health consequences of drinking lots of coffee. In one he advises a man who has just blown up at his wife to try Sanka brand. "But I like *real* coffee," the offender would peevishly protest. "Sanka *is* real coffee," the kindly Young would respond with a hearty laugh. In the next scene the former M.C.P. (that's male chauvinist pig, for you Generation Starbuckers) would be jumping up from his piece of pie and cup of Sanka to clear the table for the Missus.

By 1982, though, Young was neither young nor the ideal prescriber for a brand that wanted a long, prosperous future. The successor campaign featured physically active folks of both no and great celebrity. Underwater welder Joe Zebrosky warned of the grim consequences if he got jumpy "down here" in one ad; another (more puzzling) one showed Sanka-lovin' wedge-cut pioneer and world-famous skater Dorothy Hamill being wheeled to an airplane on a luggage cart. A print ad featuring Lena Horne promised to reveal the secret of "staying sexy," but only delivered advice about how loving yourself (and Sanka) makes you more attractive. (This is the only known instance of *Sanka* and *sexy* ever having been other than inadvertently linked.)

But by this time everybody was making ground decaffeinateds that tasted better than Sanka, General Foods included.

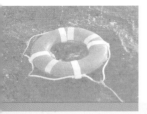

Most Popular Joke with a Sanka Punchline
What kind of coffee did they serve on the *Titanic*?

General Foods considered giving Sanka the benefit of the greatly improved decaffeination technology, but focus groups indicated that loyal users still loved Dr. Welby's medicinal brew. So the company launched the (sort of) competing Brim, Yuban, and Maxwell House decaffeinated coffees. Nowadays, Folgers and Tasters Choice Instant decaffeinateds both sell better than Sanka. But a vestige of the brand's former glory remains in the orange-rimmed coffeepots used to distinguish decaf from regular at virtually every restaurant in America.

It's natural to drink Sanka.

Sanka® is decaffeinated by a remarkable natural process that uses only pure water and nature's effervescence to wash away caffeine. With no artificial chemicals. That's why it's natural to drink Sanka® ground decaffeinated coffee.

A 1991 ad publicizing Sanka's switch from chemical to natural solvents. The natural effervescence mentioned was carbon dioxide.

No Wonder the Creamer Tasted Like Wallpaper Paste

Until complaints from consumer groups drove coffeemakers to more natural methods in the mid-1980s, Sanka and most of its competitors were decaffeinated with methylene chloride—i.e., paint stripper.

Wonder Bread

Building Strong Bodies the Bland, White-Bread Way

Bread is called the staff of life. What does it say about America that its best-selling bread is as soft as a pillow, as absorbent as a sponge, and as gaily dressed as a clown?

It says that no matter how many shuttles blow up, we still believe the products of American technology are oh-so-much-more-Wonder-ful than anything Mother Nature has been able to dream up—especially when that product so willingly lends itself to such classics as peanut butter and jelly, peanut butter and marshmallow crème, and bologna and mayonnaise.

Commercial production of white bread began shortly after the invention of the bread-wrapping machine and the motorized delivery truck at the turn of the twentieth century. Wrapping extends shelf life, and the trucks brought in the large egg, milk, and flour orders needed to make the bread and speed delivery of the final, perishable product to retail outlets. The standard size for the first loaves of prepackaged white bread all weighed 1 pound. In 1921, the Taggart Baking Company of Indianapolis innovated the market with a 1½-pound loaf they called Wonder—because no one had ever seen a commercial bread that big.

Unauthorized Uses

A small balled-up piece of crustless Wonder Bread makes a good substitute eraser. And Santa Monica artist Michael Gonzalez has used the little balls from the Wonder Bread wrappers to create a series of paintings (appropriately enough, since Gonzalez is most famous for artwork made from pieces of erasers).

TAKE A TIP FROM ME GET YOUR VITAMIN B, IN DELICIOUS WONDER BREAD

"PATENTED FLAVOR" WONDER BREAD

Wonder woman pushed the nutrition angle in the 1940s.

now! READY-SLICED **WONDER BREAD** *It's Slo-baked*

READY-SLICED *for Sandwiches*
READY-SLICED *for Toast*
READY-SLICED *for every bread use*

Within three years of this 1930 ad introducing America to sliced bread, 80 percent of all U.S. bread was sold that way.

The happy-Prozacy polka-dot bag design was reportedly inspired by the International Balloon Race held in Indianapolis. Taggart vice president Elmer Cline ordered the traffic-stopping red, blue, and yellow balloons that hovered over his home to be reproduced on the wrapper because he thought they embodied jaw-dropping Wonder (and not because—as some white bread deriders today may say—the bread was full of air or insubstantial). Taggart in 1930 was also the first company to sell sliced bread, thus giving rise to the expression, "The greatest thing since sliced bread."

During Word War II, at the U.S. government's behest, commercial breads became enriched with added iron, niacin, riboflavin, and thiamin to make up for the vitamins and minerals lost when whole wheat flour is bleached and milled into white. The government edict virtually eliminated nutritional diseases like pellagra and beriberi from the land. It also gave Wonder its nutritional advertising theme.

At first it was "Wonder helps build strong bodies 8 ways." But the ways were raised to 12 by 1961, when a TV commercial featuring the miracle of time-lapse photography showed a kid growing before boomer kids' astonished eyes. The ad was ruled deceitful by the Federal Trade Commission in 1973, and the

This famous Wonder Bread slogan debuted in the '50s.

slogan was dropped—at least for a while. (For more on that, see the box at left).

Taking nutrients out of wheat flour to make it white, then turning around and adding those nutrients back in again might sound a little crazy, not to mention expensive. But it's apparently what Americans want. Despite the natural foods movement, despite the artisan bread trend, American grocers still sell five times more white bread than all others combined—and more Wonder white than any other kind.

If at First You Don't Get Past Government Regulators, Try, Try, Again

The 1973 ruling against Wonder's "helps build strong bodies 12 ways" campaign was only the beginning of the FTC's tussles with the brand. In the late 1970s the commission charged that company boasts about the fiber content in their low-calorie Fresh Horizons bread were also deceptive because they neglected to mention that the "fiber" came not from the bread, but from added (and we would assume, yummy) wood pulp. The company dropped the Fresh Horizons ads, sales dwindled, and the product was discontinued.

In 2002, the company was once again in a hot water bath for saying that the new calcium-enriched Wonder built strong minds and bodies. The calcium ad was part of a four-year ad campaign, featuring a disheveled Professor Wonder, which actually made fun of past nutritional claims. (In one spot, he confused nutritional iron for a clothes iron.) But the unamused FTC said the company had no evidence that the bread would help anybody get into Harvard.

Although best known as white bread, Wonder has assumed many other guises.

Sacred Cellophane

In his book *The Total Package*, Thomas Hine compares the Wonder Bread wrapper to the monstrance, the container for the sacred bread in the Roman Catholic communion service. Just as the jewel-adorned monstrance calls attention to the invisible presence of Christ, the polka-dotted Wonder Bread bag calls attention to the invisible presence of the bread's unseen vitamins and minerals, Hine argues.

We don't even want to know his thoughts on wire twist ties.

Minute Maid Orange Juice
When Life Gave Them Lemons, They Made Frozen OJ

BING CROSBY says:

*For Pep,
For Vitality—
Here's the Drink
That Helps Me
Feel Young!*

Today millions can

FEEL HEALTHIER FEEL YOUNGER

with

Minute Maid
Fresh-Frozen
Orange Juice

Feel run-down? . . . old before your time? Your diet may lack protective amounts of Vitamin C and other precious vitamins and minerals in MINUTE MAID Fresh-Frozen Orange Juice.

Penny for penny, High-Vitality MINUTE MAID gives you *more* of these essential Health-Builders than even home-squeezed orange juice.

Do like Bing Crosby does—drink plenty of delicious MINUTE MAID! See if you don't feel healthier and younger, too!

Better for Your Health, Penny for Penny, than Home-Squeezed Juice!

DRINK
MINUTE MAID
...for
Better Health

Florida might still just be a vast expanse of alligator-infested swampland and we all might be squeezing our own OJ if a company with the unsexy name of the National Research Corporation hadn't begun selling frozen orange juice concentrate back in the mid-1940s.

NRC actually hadn't set out to civilize Florida or create a frozen food. They were just hoping to make a killing on a U.S. military contract for an orange juice powder to supply World War II troops. NRC proposed using the same evaporation techniques they had developed to make penicillin, and easily won the contract. But then the A-bomb hit Hiroshima, and NRC found themselves with a big new orange juice–evaporating plant and no market for the product.

Powder-produced juice simply didn't taste good enough to sell to people not stuck in foxholes, NRC vice president John Fox realized (although this did not stop General Foods marketers in 1955, as you'll see if you turn to page 67). But orange juice made from an earlier product in

(although this did not stop General Foods marketers in 1955, as you'll see if you turn to page 67).

He Should Have Stopped When He Was Ahead (of Minute Maid)

The excitement of the early days of Minute Maid gone, John Fox left Minute Maid in 1960 to become president of United Fruit, where he is credited with the idea of branding bananas with the Chiquita sticker. Other fruit companies soon followed suit. Forgetful people who have chowed down on an apple only to find themselves also inadvertently eating a paper label now know whom to blame.

An orange doubles as an ornament on this company holiday card.

Bing Crosby and Little Miss Minute Maid shared brand spokesperson duties in the late 1940s.

Food Formalwear

Minute Maid orange juice debuted in vertically oriented cans covered with oranges. But by 1964, with most of the competition featuring similar citrus designs, the company decided to go with something completely different: a label that was predominantly black.

Black, of course, has been traditionally associated with death, and conventional package-design thinking held that products cloaked in it would suffer a similar fate. But black was also the color of limousines, tuxedos, and expensive stereo equipment, in whose rarified air Minute Maid wanted to be considered.

Long story short: The gamble worked so well that by the mid-1990s Minute Maid was compelled to return to images of oranges in order to stand out from all the food products that had copied their black packaging.

the powder-making process—frozen orange juice concentrate—did taste pretty good. So he decided to concentrate on the concentrate.

The first frozen orange juices were full-strength products produced by a number of small companies (including one headed by Richard M. Nixon) in the mid- to late 1930s. They had only modest success (the frozen juice being heavy and expensive to ship). The concentrate process was developed by government scientists in the mid-'40s, and was pioneered as a retail product in supermarkets by Snow Crop in 1945. But NRC enjoyed even greater success and developed the concentrate formula that became the industry standard.

Then based in Boston, NRC hired a local ad agency that came up with the name Minute Maid, an allusion to the local Revolutionary War Minutemen as well as to how quickly the juice could be "made" by maidens (rather than men). In 1949, the brand name was brought to life by Little Miss Minute Maid, a cartoon baby sporting a Scotch plaid bonnet to extol the economy of frozen concentrate and the virtues of serving Minute Maid to babies.

This overloaded symbol has been almost entirely forgotten in the wake of the company's two long-term ad campaigns featuring singer-actor Bing Crosby. The low-key Crosby was the perfect spokesman for this still-new and skeptically viewed frozen food. "I'll buy your first can of Minute Maid," Bing promised in a 1949 ad that was used to encourage customers in new markets. The ad also made a lot of people think he owned the company (recently renamed Minute Maid, after their orange juice)—and they weren't far wrong. Crosby had only agreed to do the initial batch of 15-minute, 5-day-a-week radio shows for 20,000 shares of Minute Maid stock. (Maybe that's why he never appeared to break a sweat in any of his performances.) Crosby's clout with the company was so great that when they asked him to come back for a new series of TV commercials in 1968, they agreed

Minute Maid's New Year's Day parade through Pasadena.

Question:	*Answer:*
Why does Frank Gifford *crave* Orange Juice after a tough game?	His Body Wisdom tells him he needs extra Vitamin C and quick energy!

Frank Gifford scores some Minute Maid.

to his request that they star his aspiring-actor kids.

Whether because of Crosby or the product quality he was forever boasting about, Minute Maid Orange Juice Concentrate was a huge success. Within 10 years of its introduction in 1946, sales rose from $374,000 to $106.5 million, spawning dozens of competitors. Frozen concentrate's popularity also helped the Florida orange market grow from a small, highly seasonal business to an economic powerhouse that, together with World War II military bases and the tourism industry, virtually made the state of Florida. As the first large-volume frozen food in the supermarket, frozen orange juice also gave grocers their best reason yet to install the freezers that would eventually yield a bounty of Stouffer's Macaroni and Cheese, Sara Lee Pound Cake, and Ben & Jerry's Ice Cream.

Sales of ready-made orange juice in the refrigerator case overtook sales of frozen in 1985. Increasingly busy (and lazy?) Americans no longer wanted to wait for the frozen yellow logs to dissolve in water. But if you count refrigerated orange juice that is made from frozen concentrate at the factory, the frozen juice that Minute Maid helped innovate still accounts for almost 70 percent of all the orange juice Americans drink.

Maybe Not "The Best There Is." But Better Than You Probably Think
In these days of calcium-enriched, vitamin-fortified, choose-your-amount-of-pulp not-from-concentrate, orange juice created from a frozen can may seem about as quaint as family musicales and handwritten letters. And yet a 2002 study by scientists at Arizona State University in Mesa showed that orange juice from frozen concentrate had significantly higher amounts of the all-important vitamin C than its ready-to-drink counterparts (86 milligrams versus as low as 27 for ready-to-drink) and also retained these higher amounts much longer.

Frozen concentrates have also beaten out many more expensive juices in taste tests conducted by *Consumer Reports* and *Cook's Illustrated* magazines. In *Consumer's* 1995 report, Minute Maid frozen concentrate came in behind only fresh-squeezed and Minute Maid's own not-from-concentrate refrigerated high-pulp product, and was rated a Best Buy. In addition to the cost savings of as much as 30 percent, frozen concentrate fans cite refrigerator space savings.

In other words, it just might be time to dig out that Tupperware pitcher.

Bac-Os
Soy Prodigy

Bac-Os bacon-flavor bits are the supermarket's quiet misfit: highly artificial and dated—but too little known to attract even ridicule. Even as new soy-based foods register double-digit sales gains, Bac-Os remain largely unheralded. As the only survivor of a whole line of soy products General Mills once made, Bac-Os may just be a too-painful reminder of a $60-million mistake some older executives would just as soon forget.

In 1959 General Mills began spending around $3 million a year to turn soybeans

BAC*OS® ARE NATIONAL — Bac*Os, the first of the BONTRAE® textured vegetable protein foods being sold to homemakers, are now available nationally. Recently the uses for Bac*Os and other products in the BONTRAE line, manufactured and sold by the newly formed Food Service and Protein Products Division, were filmed for possible use in a CBS-TV News story on foods of the future. Gene Monroe, Technician, Food Service and Protein Products Division, left, demonstrates one of the uses for Bac*Os under the eye of a CBS News film camera.

Bac-Os, a 1970 food of the future.

into imitation beef, chicken, ham, and sausage products under the Bontrae label. Bac-Os bits were the first of these to hit supermarkets. They consisted of dough made from soy flour that was cooked and stretched on extruding machines (similar to those used to make cereal) to give them their crisp texture. Added oil, salt, sugar, and flavors lent the nearly flavorless soy bits their smoky flavor; caramel, their color.

"Textured protein foods are a revolution in consumer

Spinoffs

General Mills also made Saus-Os (sausage-flavored) and Pepr-Os (pepperoni-flavored) soy bits for a time in the early 1970s before poor sales led to their demise. Could names that sounded like a drunkard and a remedy for pepperoni-induced indigestion, respectively, have had anything to do with it?

products, offering the ultimate in convenience because there is no preparation required and because they can be stored in the cupboard, without refrigerating, even after opening," enthused the May 1968 General Mills newsletter announcing Bac-Os bits' national debut. A subsequent edition

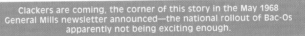

Clackers are coming, the corner of this story in the May 1968 General Mills newsletter announced—the national rollout of Bac-Os apparently not being exciting enough.

reported on Bac-Os bits' prominent role in a CBS news story about "Foods of the Future."

But the first consumer magazine ads for Baco-Os aimed to reassure more than impress. With Betty Crocker's familiar name and face front and center, they explained that Bac-Os bits needed no frying or refrigeration and could "do wonderful things" for sauces, dips, vegetables, and soups. Later, even more innocuous ads talked about the crunch Bac-Os bits could impart to salads. But just how many salad lovers feel vegetables are not complete unless complemented by the taste of meat (if not actual meat)? And how many people are concerned enough about bacon's nutritional faults to seek out an alternative?

General Mills might have also been wrong in thinking that people wanted their kitchens to be nothing more than a storage space for perfectly shaped, perfectly healthy, premade foods. Even now that soy's health benefits are well known, real cholesterol-laden bacon-bit products still sell just as well as imitation ones like Bac-Os.

Pop Question

Q: Can Bac-Os bits stop hot flashes, lower cholesterol, prevent osteoporosis, and prevent cancer?

A: Soy reportedly can help do these things, and Bac-Os do contain soy. But a 1.5-tablespoon serving of Bac-Os contains only 3 grams of soy. That means you'd have to eat at least half a bottle a day in order to begin to reap some of these reported health benefits.

You can get the same effect from drinking a couple of glasses of soy milk or munching a third of a cup of soy nuts, but life sustained this way would obviously not be worth living.

Beer Nuts
Blue-collar Redskins

How did a candy shop kiddy snack become one of America's most beloved bar treats?

In the 1940s, Russell Shirk of the Caramel Crisp candy shop of Bloomington, Illinois, was selling his "slightly sweet, lightly salted" redskin peanuts alongside the shop's signature orange drink, when a customer who happened also to be a potato chip distributor asked if he could try selling them on his route.

Eldredge C. Brewster had only modest success selling Shirk's Glazed Peanuts to grocery stores, but they took off with tavern owners because they made customers thirsty for more beer. So Shirk and Brewster decided to change the name of the product to Beer Nuts one day in 1953 (probably over a beer). No focus group or marketing firm was consulted. If they had, Shirk and Brewster might have thought twice about a name that makes some people think the nuts are boiled in beer (they're not) and makes others think they can't be eaten with anything but (wrong again).

The Most Famous Beer Nuts Joke

Q: What's the difference between Beer Nuts and deer nuts?

A: Beer Nuts cost about a dollar; deer nuts are under a buck.

Just a few of the teams who proudly call themselves Beer Nuts.

The Beer Nuts family now includes sweet 'n salty cashews and almonds.

They also might have anticipated some of the thousands of jokes that would result from a product name that contains a slang expression for a part of the male anatomy.

What Shirk and Brewster couldn't have anticipated was Mothers Against Drunk Driving, the fear of fat (which accounts for 80 to 90 percent of roasted peanuts, "good" fat though it may be), the decline of the neighborhood bar, and the related rise of the brewpub, which serves its own food and so has no interest in giving any away. Worst of all was how big snack-food companies like Eagle and Planters came out with similar products in the late 1970s—although the younger generation of Shirks who now run the company don't see them as similar.

For one thing, the sugar and salt on those other products are slathered on in a way that masks the nuts' flavor, whereas the top-secret Beer Nuts process delicately cooks it in. Beer Nut peanuts also retain their skins, which adds a slightly bitter taste to their much more complex mix of sugar, salt, and fat, they say.

In other words, the Shirks talk about Beer Nuts the same snooty way microbrewers and brewpub owners talk about beer.

The Shirks' new Web site positions Beer Nuts as a cult product with a merchandise catalog full of Beer Nut T-shirts and mugs and a Beer Nut of the Month Club, for people nutty enough to spend $17 a month for Beer Nuts bags that cost about $5 at the drugstore.

But the old-fashioned Beer Nuts red-and-white logo, motorcycle and auto racing sponsorships, and online testimonials ("I fell asleep on a sunny raft after a beer and Beer Nut lunch and woke up the color of Beer Nuts, yada, yada") tell a different story.

Starring Beer Nuts

Beer Nuts have been extolled (or derided) by everyone from Drew Carey to David Letterman to Murphy Brown. But the show most associated with the brand is *Cheers*. Norm Peterson once punctuated some wisdom about women by saying, "Pass the Beer Nuts." And one advertising campaign for the show simply pictured Sam, Norm, Cliff, and company, and the words "Beer Nuts."

Philadelphia Cream Cheese
A Little Taste of New York State

It's a bagel's best friend, the brick that launched a million cheesecakes, and, like jazz and paint-on-velvet, one of America's important contributions to world culture—although Philadelphia Cream Cheese has almost nothing to do with Philadelphia.

Cream cheese was invented by New York State dairyman William A. Lawrence in the late 1800s. His aim was to try to make an American (i.e., fattier) version of the French Neufchatel cheese—a mild cheese made of milk and cream (hence the name *cream cheese*). The process was pretty standard cheesemaking; the difference was the greater richness of ingredients. The brand name *Philadelphia* was adopted by one Lawrence customer who was hoping to trade on Philadelphia's fame as a home of fine dairy products. (This was obviously way before Philadelphia became famous for its Cheez Whiz–topped cheesesteaks.)

The bogus Philadelphia connection was one way the Phenix cheese company tried to distinguish itself from Lawrence's other cream cheese clients. Another was to emphasize the brand's freshness. (As the best-selling brand, it moved out of stores the fastest, the early ads argued.) After Phenix merged with Kraft in 1928, Philadelphia brand also had the benefit of Kraft pasteurization techniques, which eventually lengthened Philadelphia's shelf life from two days to four weeks.

The company initially suggested using Philly in easy and economical (if not incredibly enticing) desserts made by spreading the cheese on crackers with jam or slices of fruit, and as a whipped cream substitute. One 1930 ad advised slathering Philadelphia Cream Cheese on day-old bread to create a sandwich loaf. But "Cream cheese for breakfast? Whoever heard of that?" was the prevailing view espoused in one 1931 ad before it boldly suggested trying Philly and jam on toast.

Cooking with Philly really got creative in the '40s and '50s, thanks to the *Kraft Television Theatre,* a live drama series interrupted by long ads featuring Kraft recipes. The ads starred anonymous female hands preparing the food and were narrated with mouth-watering enthusiasm by Ed Herlihy—so enthusiastic, in fact, that 24 hours after Herlihy told *Kraft Television Theatre*

viewers how to make a clam appetizer dip with Philadelphia Cream Cheese, there wasn't a can of clams to be found in all of Manhattan.

Philadelphia Cream Cheese recipes for hot crab dip, no-bake fudge, frosting, pie crust, and cheesecake introduced on the show also became middle-American kitchen classics—none more so than the cheesecake. Despite the bagel's large contribution to increases in recent cream cheese sales, cheesecake has remained the focus of most company promotions.

An old hand passes along some cream cheese wisdom in this 1942 ad.

Sophisticated
Meat Balls

Meat balls in the gourmet class? You do it with famous Philadelphia Brand Cream Cheese.

Combine 1 lb. ground beef, ⅓ c. dry bread crumbs, ⅓ c. milk, 1 egg, 2 tbsps. chopped onion, ½ tsp. Worcestershire, ½ tsp. salt, dash pepper. Shape into balls and brown in Kraft Oil. Cover and cook 15 minutes.

Remove balls, pour off drippings and stir in 1 can condensed mushroom soup, an 8-oz. Philadelphia Brand Cream Cheese cubed (be sure it's this guaranteed-fresh brand) and ½ c. water. Mix until well blended and heat. Serve meat balls and sauce on hot noodles.

See The Andy Williams Show, Monday nights, NBC TV

PHILADELPHIA CREAM CHEESE
KRAFT

Look for this famous name in the oval. Guaranteed-Fresh when you buy it or your money back.

"Meat balls in the gourmet class" made with cream of mushroom soup and Philadelphia cream cheese in 1965.

On Valentine's Day 1997, for instance, Kraft celebrated the fiftieth anniversary of the famous Philadelphia 3-Step Cheesecake recipe with a party at New York's Penn Station. It featured actors dressed as cupids, couples celebrating 50 years of marriage, and a 6-foot-long cheesecake that was then delivered to the brand's namesake city (now the product's fourth best-selling market behind Baltimore, Cincinnati, and Boston) on a train wrapped in Mylar to resemble Philly's trademark foil-wrapped package.

In keeping with the brand's wacky promotion tradition and their new indulgent "Taste of Heaven" ad theme, their hugely successful premade cheesecake snack bars were introduced in Chicago, Boston, Detroit, and five other cities in 2000 by dozens of halo- and wing-clad "angels" bearing baskets of free samples.

Philadelphia 3-Step Cheesecake

2 8-ounce packages Philadelphia Cream Cheese, softened
½ cup sugar
½ teaspoon vanilla
2 eggs
1 6-ounce graham piecrust

Mix cream cheese, sugar, and vanilla with electric mixer on medium speed until blended. Add eggs; mix until blended. Pour into crust. Bake at 325°F for 40 minutes or until center is almost set. Cool. Refrigerate 3 hours or overnight. Refrigerate leftover cheesecake. Serves 8.

Carnation Instant Breakfast
Solid Food Is Overrated

This 1967 ad visually spelled out the breakfast-in-a-glass concept.

In the early 1960s, Carnation food scientists in Van Nuys, California, decided to come up with a new product in response to surveys that found busy Americans were no longer eating breakfast together, if they ate it at all.

Working at a dairy company, they immediately thought of fortifying milk with even more vitamins and minerals (which wasn't a particularly new idea). But to make a glass of milk the nutritional equivalent of the full, wholesome breakfast that nobody had time for, to make milk a meal, as they proposed—why, this was a revolutionary concept.

If the idea was interesting, the rebus-style ads designed to sell it were brilliant. They pictured two eggs, two strips of bacon, toast, and juice on one side, and a single frosty glass of chocolate milk positioned on the other side to show that it contained the total nourishment of a traditional American breakfast. For jaw-dropping impressiveness, these ads rivaled watching the Wonder Bread kid grow.

As many as 20 women in a company of 20,000 workers will faint on the job each week because they're not eating a good breakfast, reported the Carnation company newsletter, *The Carnation,* in an April 1965 article touting their latest product. Even those who do eat breakfast sometimes worry if it is big or varied enough to give them the proper nutrients, Carnation vice president Mark Shackelford noted in another company story. Carnation Instant Breakfast "takes the worry out of breakfast" and provides variety in the form of multiple flavors: initially plain, chocolate, and coffee, but before long, also chocolate malted, banana, eggnog, and strawberry.

Tearing open these envelopes and stirring them into a glass of cold milk was also truly instant and efficient, certainly compared to making bacon and eggs, Shackelford

A BODY COULDN'T ASK FOR ANYTHING MORE

Just light enough.
Just sweet and smooth enough.
A breakfast with just enough balanced nutrition—protein, minerals, vitamins and food energy —to keep a body beautiful. That's Carnation Instant Breakfast mixed with milk. Comes in lots of tantalizing flavors.
No body could ask for anything more.

CARNATION INSTANT BREAKFAST

Diet product or fashion spread? Neither. It's a 1968 ad for Carnation Instant Breakfast.

continued: "Nothing is wasted and there are no dirty dishes" (not counting the glass, obviously). What's more, Carnation Instant Breakfast's initial estimated cost was only 19 cents per glass, including milk; this was a lot cheaper than the same nutrients consumed in the form of bacon, eggs, toast, and fruit.

For the first time in company history, Carnation's entire sales force was assembled at the February 1965 regional meetings where Carnation Instant Breakfast was crowned King of the Mardi Gras. Carnation realized it would take all their powers of persuasion to convince grocers that Carnation Instant Breakfast would not hurt cereal sales but would instead appeal to a whole new audience of survey-identified, mostly-young breakfast skippers.

Before long millions of young consumers were standing at

the kitchen counter gulping down a glass before running off to the bus stop or class. What kid could resist a chocolate shake for breakfast? Ads from the late '60s and early '70s showed female will-'o-the-wisps in mod clothes drinking the presumably equally mod Carnation Instant Breakfast. In fact, for many teenage girls and young women, Instant Breakfast doubled as a diet drink, at least until diet drinks like Slim-Fast came along in the mid- to late 1970s.

Diet powder drinks delivered the first blow to Instant Breakfast sales. The second came in the '90s from energy drinks like Red Bull and energy bars like Clif, which, with their herbal ingredients and soy, made Instant Breakfast's vitamins and minerals in milk seem almost Stone Age.

Carnation has tried to keep up with the times by boosting calcium (when it was publicized as an osteoporosis fighter) and introducing Instant Breakfast in the even-more-instant ready-to-drink cans. In the last few years, a number of consumer and health magazines have declared old Carnation Instant Breakfast at least as good nutritionally as (and cheaper and better-tasting than) the newfangled competition. Certainly almost everyone would now agree that Instant Breakfast is better nutritionally than the bacon-and-eggs breakfast it was originally meant to replace.

Instant Breakfast Ice Cream

1 packet Carnation Instant Breakfast, any flavor (though vanilla tastes best)
1 cup milk

Mix Instant Breakfast with milk; put in a plastic container in the freezer until soft-frozen. Pulse in blender until mixture reaches an ice cream (or ice milk) consistency. Serves 1.

Chapter 4

INDESTRUCTIBLES
AND RECYCLABLES

We live in turbulent times. Favorite TV shows and high-flying companies are gone in the blink of an eye or with the help of a well-timed lawsuit. So what lasts? What can you count on? Foods that, for reasons of popularity or preservatives, will be around long after you and I are gone.

Most foods spoil—unless it's one of the foods in this chapter, whose manufacturers have, through technology, altered this perfectly natural process. Other products you see here have been preserved in another way: They've been made from scraps of food that would otherwise be thrown away. They're examples of food companies doing an environmentally responsible thing for their own selfish reasons.

Carnation Instant Nonfat Dry Milk
Magic Crystals from Contented Cows

Milk is a hard enough sell even in its full-fat form (why do you think the dairy industry is paying celebrities to wear milk mustaches?). But talking up skim milk created by mixing water and white powder is not something to be attempted without a large plate of freshly baked chocolate chip cookies, even if instant dry milk does keep in the cupboard for months rather than fresh milk's days, and even though the instant nonfat dried milk now sold is a taste treat compared to the one sold in the 1940s.

Back in those pre-instant days, the powder caked in the box and didn't totally combine with the water in the glass. In other words, it looked curdled. Those who were able to choke down a whole glass of this semi-liquid were rewarded with the sight of bottom-of-the-glass sludge.

It took a war—with its fresh-milk shortages—to make this stuff popular.

This 1954 introductory ad enlisted the concept of "magic crystals" to distinguish new Carnation Instant milk from the old, clumping kinds.

What's in a Name?

HELLO E. A. Stuart called his Kent, Washington, company *Carnation* to suggest the freshness and sweetness of the evaporated milk products he began making in 1899. Certainly his milk was a lot fresher and sweeter than the Carnation brand cigars that initially inspired the product name.

Spinoff

Carnation Instant Chocolate Flavor Drink was introduced a year after regular instant powdered milk. It was a big flop, but it laid the technological groundwork for a whole host of successful hot cocoa mixes by Carnation and competitors like Swiss Miss.

In 1953, milk and ice cream maker Carnation decided to cash in on the residual market of cheapskates who continued to use dried milk for baking even after affordable liquid milk had made its postwar comeback. The company was all set to launch Carnation Dried Milk in cake-resistant jars when a box of a new dried milk then being sold in Sacramento found its way into the company's test kitchens. Conventional methods of drying milk involve evaporating, concentrating, and then spray-drying the milk in a container filled with hot air so that it forms a powder. But Northern California milk processor Dave Peebles's idea of leaving a little water in with the powder before spray-drying greatly improved the milk's solubility.

"I was . . . overwhelmed," said kitchen director Virginia Piper of her first encounter with Peebles Instant Nonfat Milk. "The sight of those magic crystals drifting down from the surface of the water and becoming a homogenous product with just a stir or two was phenomenal, like discovering that Christmas was every day of the

Instant Nonfat Milk creator Dave Peebles.

A model at Carnation Instant's 1954 launch with her hands (and lap) full of protein-rich foods.

year," said Piper (who clearly took her job very seriously).

And so Carnation dumped all 100,000 cases of its formerly new powdered milk like so much bulk trash and struck a deal with Mr. Peebles.

Introductory ads for the new Carnation Instant Nonfat Dry Milk Solids were almost as enthusiastic as Piper. "Miracle dairy product," screamed one full-page treatise. "Not a powder, not a flake—only Carnation has magic crystals that burst into delicious nonfat milk!" "Hot [milk] with no boilovers, no skin." Cold with "no lumps or leftover paste," read another in a series that featured anonymous kids with the milk mustaches that would later show up on Mark McGwire and Ray Charles.

U.S. sales for nonfat powered milk peaked in the early 1960s, or at about the same time Carnation had recovered the cost of this massive ad blitz.

This is the Instant that's delicious for drinking!

Carnation
INSTANT
NONFAT

A 1958 Carnation milk mustache kid who appears to be tripping on tryptophan.

Today the vast majority of powdered milk is served up surreptitiously in commercial puddings, pies, and other baked goods as well as by people who water down their orange juice and eagerly scarf down thrift-shop donuts.

Twinkies
Twinkie, Twinkie, Junk-Food Star

Once people had to make any cake they ate—or at least haul themselves down to the local bakery. Now you can buy snack cakes at every grocery and convenience store, in many vending machines —even at gas stations.

And the cakes we buy most often are Twinkies.

Just how popular are Twinkies? During the great Hostess Teamsters strike of 2000, desperate Twinkie fans paid up to $5,000 for boxes of the edible sponges on eBay. A house in Kennett Square, Pennsylvania, was burglarized twice in one year solely for its Twinkies. Twinkies were one of the few foods included in the official U.S. millennium time capsule (and when it's opened in 2100, it will probably be the only food still good to eat).

Twinkie inventor Jimmy Dewar.

Twinkies are also beloved by baboons. (Could it be yet another sign of their close kinship with man?) A group of these highly social primates escaped from a zoo in Kings Mill, Ohio, in 1976 and were recaptured only after someone got the bright idea of luring them into a cage with some Twinkies.

Like anything so much in the public eye (or, in this case, the public's stomachs), Twinkies have also been greatly maligned: as the food that fueled the 1979 shooting spree that killed San Francisco mayor George Moscone and city supervisor Harvey Milk, and as a bribe a Minneapolis politician used to get the senior citizen vote.

Dan White was acquitted of murder charges in the Moscone and Milk case, and found guilty only on the lesser charge of voluntary manslaughter; his lawyer argued that White's mental capacities had been impaired by his high intake of Twinkies, potato chips, and Coca-Cola. And yet that legal argument is now known as the Twinkie defense.

In 1985, when Minneapolis city council candidate George Belair feted senior citizens groups with a $34.13 spread of coffee, Kool-Aid, doughnuts, cookies, Ho Hos, and Twinkies, the ensuing scandal likewise was widely known as Twinkiegate—not Kool-Aidgate or Ho Hogate.

Why are Twinkies getting all the blame? Could it be their unusual shape?

Twinkies were invented by Hostess Chicago plant manager Jimmy Dewar in 1930 as a way to make more efficient use of shortcake pans that were used only during the six-week strawberry season. But have you ever seen shortcake—or any other food, for that matter—that looks like Twinkies? (No wonder the aliens in *Blue Man Group: Tubes* spend so much of their long-running off-Broadway show puzzling over it.)

Twinkie's 70th birthday cake was made from 20,000 Twinkies.

A petition from teenager Judd Slivka helped get Twinkie the Kid back on packages in 1990.

Dewar was reportedly inspired to name the new treat *Twinkies* by a billboard advertising Twinkle Toe Shoes. Dewar may be alone in thinking the part of the anatomy Twinkies most closely resembles are toes, but since he was the boss, what he thought counted.

Much merriment has also been made of Twinkies' indestructibility. The treat is widely believed to have the shelf life of nuclear waste and the resiliency of foam rubber. In fact, when

So Now Tell Us Something We Don't Already Know

The largest number of Twinkie eaters live in downscale rural communities and are more likely than other Americans to enjoy chewing tobacco, professional wrestling, country music, aerosol cheese, bacon, Kool-Aid, and malt liquor. They are also pretty much oblivious to the idea of health food and fitness, according to Michael J. Weiss's 1994 book, *Latitudes & Attitudes*.

Some Say His Fried Mars Bars Are Even Better

Compared with all the other packaged baked goods gussied up with frosting, nuts, and sprinkles, a Twinkie's simple combination of golden sponge cake and sweet crème is positively demure. Unless, of course, you fry the Twinkie, sprinkle it with confectioners' sugar, and serve it on a bed of la-dee-da four-berry coulis the way Christopher Sell does. Since the Brooklyn fish and chip shop owner invented this startling new Twinkie preparation, a further innovation of fried Twinkies-on-a-stick have become a state fair staple. Their taste has been compared to a Krispy Kreme doughnut (in case you want to know what you're going to get for going to all the trouble).

some Rice University students threw a Twinkie off a six-story building as a part of a battery of scientific tests documented by their Tests with Inorganic Noxious Kakes in Extreme Situations (T.W.I.N.K.I.E.S.), it suffered only a minor fissure. (Check out the project Web site at www.twinkiesproject.com.)

Twinkies would also appear to be as far as one could possibly get from the hearty fruits, vegetables, grains, and legumes that are all the rage among nutrition experts these days. The Twinkie is, in fact, the quintessential symbol of American junk food. And yet Twinkie lovers show impressive longevity. Inventor Dewar ate three a day and lived to 88. Lewis Browning, 87, of Shelbyville, Indiana, has eaten at least one Twinkie a day since 1941 and is still living to spread the good news. Twinkies were also a favorite food of Mary Christian, who was America's oldest citizen until her death in April 2003 at age 113.

It must be the preservatives.

Fancy fried Twinkies.

Fried Twinkies

10 Twinkies	Flour for dusting
1 1/8 cups flour	Powdered sugar
1 tablespoon malt vinegar	1 cup frozen raspberries
1 teaspoon baking powder	1 cup frozen blackberries
1 teaspoon salt	1 cup frozen strawberries
1 1/2 cups water	1 cup frozen blueberries
Oil for frying	4 tablespoons sugar

Cool Twinkies in refrigerator. Whisk together 1 cup flour with vinegar, baking powder, salt, and water until batter is consistency of custard. Heat oil in a deep fryer to 400°F. Roll each Twinkie in remaining flour, then roll in batter. Drop battered Twinkie in the fryer for about 90 seconds, until the outside is golden brown and the filling starts to melt. Top with powdered sugar, cut in half on the bias, and serve with four-berry coulis.

To make the coulis: Put berries into a pan on low heat and add sugar. When the mixture begins to boil, put in a blender and then strain the seeds through a sieve. Serves 10.

SPAM

Egg, Bacon, Sausage, and Spam; Spam, Egg, Spam, Spam; Spam, Spam, Spam, Spam, Spam, Spam, Baked Beans, and Spam

How do people find Spam funny? Let us count the ways:

1. Its perky pink color.
2. Its distinctive smell and taste.
3. Its perfectly rectangular shape.
4. The name, which screams of something like but not quite ham.

In sum, in this era of pure and natural foods, Spam luncheon meat is canned laughter as much as canned meat.

Which itself is funny (in the ironic rather than the ha-ha way) considering Spam's original, quite serious business aims. In the mid-1930s virtually all meat products were sold either fresh or only slightly preserved. That put them at the mercy of market prices and seasonal slaughtering schedules and in direct competition with meats made by every other company. Geo. A. Hormel Company president Jay Hormel believed that canned meats would solve those problems, which is why, in 1926, he hired German canning expert Paul Joern to help him produce the country's first canned ham. Their chief technical challenge was to keep the meat's cell walls from giving up too much fluid under the heat of canning. Joern eventually solved the problem by adding salt, finding the proper cooking time, and sucking the air out of the can to create a vacuum.

When competitors copied, Hormel got the even better idea of blending ham and spices with what had previously been a nearly worthless piece of hog

Gracie Allen and George Burns hammed it up for radio show sponsor Spam in 1940.

A unique recipe idea from the late 1940s.

meat in a vacuum (to prevent the same excess juice problem they'd had with ham), canning it, and marketing the heck out of it. The Depression created a ready audience of budget-strapped house-wives who proudly served a clove-studded square of Spam for Sunday dinner instead of the more expensive baked ham.

Spam's affordability and near indestructibility also made it popular with armed forces purchasing offices during World War II. It was less so with soldiers; they called it "ham that didn't pass its physical" and "meat loaf without basic training." But for every vet who swore he would never eat Spam again, there were at least two who became Spam fans as a result of their wartime initiation; because of them, Spam sales after the war really took off.

One of a series of call-and-response cartoon balloon ads that launched Spam in the late 1930s.

The World War II GI jokes, cartoons, and poems also marked the beginning of Spam's life as a cultural icon. Three decades later the Monty Python skit about a restaurant with an all-Spam menu made Spam seem funny to the next generation of Americans and Brits. That bit, in turn, inspired the Internet term *spamming*, which refers to unsolicited e-mail messages that—like the Spam in the Python's Green Midget Café—are ubiquitous.

Spam continues to be popular with the rapidly dwindling

One Reason the Yankees Won the 1998 World Series
Guess what kept Cuban pitcher Orlando Hernandez alive during his December 1997 sea flight to freedom and a $6.6-million Yankees contract? A leaky sailboat stocked only with water, sugar, bread, and four cans of Spam.

World War II generation and in places where U.S. troops have been stationed, including Hawaii, Guam, and Korea. Spam sushi—made by topping a fried slab of Spam with a block of sticky rice and wrapping them together with a belt of seaweed—is as common to convenience stores and takeout joints in Hawaii as hot dogs are to these same places on the mainland. Car dealers in Guam lure buyers by filling new car trunks with Spam. In Korea, gift-givers without a clue turn to $35- to $75-gift packages of Spam as eagerly as Americans turn to Hickory Farms, Godiva, or Dewar's.

Hormel says that Spam is still regularly purchased by more than 25 percent of U.S. households. But Spam now fuels at least as much frivolity as it does metabolisms. That frivolity includes the Spamarama cookoff and Spamalympics (or Pigathlon) held annually in Austin, Texas, on the weekend closest to April Fool's Day, and the likewise-unauthorized Spam Haiku Archive, Church of Spam, and Spam Cam Web sites.

After years of legal sparring with Spam pranksters, Hormel has recently discovered a sense of humor (or Spam's non-food profit potential) in, among other things, a Spam merchandise catalog that offers Spam flip-flops and boxers, and a 16,500-square-foot Spam Museum featuring a Spam factory worker dress-up trunk, a replica of the Green Midget Café, and mannequins of Jay Hormel and his dad arguing about the business.

The Spam NASCAR race car and driver Lake Speed, circa 1995.

Sons of SPAM

None of Spam inventor Jay Hormel's three sons went into the family business that made them millionaires. But two of them have become almost as famous as Spam. George "Geordie" Hormel is a composer and musician who produced records for Fleetwood Mac, the Rolling Stones, and Frank Zappa. His younger brother James is America's first openly gay U.S. ambassador—to Luxembourg. (After that gays-in-the-military fiasco, who can blame Bill Clinton for wanting to start small?)

Unauthorized Uses

World War II soldiers used Spam to soften their hands, grease their guns, and waterproof their boots. Some fishermen say it makes great bait (especially for catfish and carp). Comic Jack Swersie has made a career of juggling Spam (both in and outside of the can). And at least some x-ray techs use Spam as a magnetic resonance imaging (MRI) marker.

Techs traditionally have used butter or Crisco to help draw physicians' attention to a problem area. But Craig Yoder of Hemet Valley Medical Center in California says Spam shows up better, doesn't melt from body heat, and also comes in handy when he forgets his lunch.

Velveeta
All-American Hunk

Velveeta really doesn't deserve this spot next to Spam and Twinkies. Its foil-wrapped industrial-sized loaves and highway construction cone hue notwithstanding, Velveeta was invented to be a more nutritious alternative to natural cheese.

This 1941 kid likes Velveeta's flavor; his mom, its nutrition.

Regular cheese is made by introducing bacteria into milk, then letting the milk solids (called *curd*) spoil. (Be glad I spared you the part about calf's stomachs.) The milk liquids that are also produced during this process, called *whey*, are thrown away, along with many of the nutrients milk contains. Velveeta was the result of Kraft's high-minded desire to stuff this nutritious whey back into cheese.

"A miracle wrought with milk," Kraft proclaimed in one 1927 introductory ad. "Through the aid of scientific research, we are at last able to combine in a cheese product all those precious health-giving qualities of the rich whole milk."

The result was not only a more nutritious cheese, but also one that was softer than cheddar and as smooth as velvet (hence the name). At room temperature, it was as creamy as butter. When chilled, it would slice. It also melted easily and had a mild taste. The pasteurization (and later, preservatives) that was Kraft's calling card gave it a longer shelf life than "natural"

Let Them Eat Velveeta

The Food and Drug Administration has already banned sales of raw milk cheeses that haven't been aged for at least 60 days. In mid-2003, officials hinted that they might begin imposing restrictions on any cheese made from unpasteurized milk. The concern is that these cheeses might be hotbeds of salmonella, listeria, and *E. coli.* In other words, Velveeta and its pasteurized cousins, Cheez Whiz and Kraft Singles, could soon be America's sole legal cheese currency.

cheese. Because of these differences, it was called cheese food. From Day 1, the box proudly bore the phrase.

Within a few years Kraft had funded a research program at Rutgers University to independently confirm Velveeta's nutritional superiority. (Yes, back in 1930 some lucky scientist was able to go to a party and say that he was a research fellow in Velveeta cheese.) In fact, much of what nutritional science knows about riboflavin can be traced back to the Velveeta studies, which is a little bit scary, considering some of Rutgers' methodology. To measure Velveeta's ability "to support muscular work," for instance, test subjects rode stationary bicycles while wearing huge metal buckets dubbed "respiration helmets."

All the money Kraft was investing in research paid off when Velveeta received the American Medical Association's endorsement. Among other things, the AMA asserted that Velveeta's protein was "complete for the building of firm flesh." (Velveeta does, in fact, have one-third fewer calories than cheddar.)

Cartoon-style ads translated the science for consumers. In one ad from 1938 a father tells his bicep-proud son to "keep eating what Mother says and be an All-American one day." The next panel shows Sonny at his mother's knee, listening with rapt attention as she reads aloud Velveeta's scientific claims.

But Velveeta ads more typically feature recipes. The enduring classics include Velveeta-made grilled cheese sandwiches, macaroni and cheese, tuna noodle casserole, and party dips made by combining Velveeta with chili, spinach, or salsa.

Velveeta has actually been superseded in many of these uses by other, newer Kraft products. It's now quicker and easier to make a

Smooth-melting Velveeta will give you a prize inspiration

The cheese food that's digestible as milk itself!

The same Velveeta-loving kid in 1935.

All in the Family
One of the offspring of the 1980 marriage between Kraft and Tupperware-maker Dart Industries was a Tupperware Velveeta Keeper.

grilled cheese with Kraft Singles, macaroni and cheese with Kraft Macaroni & Cheese, and a cheese dip with Cheez Whiz, for instance. But only Velveeta can do it all while still leaving room in your refrigerator for something besides Kraft cheese.

Queso Dip

Dallas Morning News writer Teresa Gubbins says this absurdly easy dip is de rigueur even at the fanciest parties and toniest restaurants in Texas (i.e., ones that offer cloth napkins with their ribs). It's also a favorite of former President Bill Clinton.

1 1-pound loaf Velveeta, cubed
1 10-ounce can Ro-Tel diced tomatoes and green chiles

In a heavy saucepan, combine cheese cubes and Ro-Tel tomatoes; stir over low heat until cheese melts. Serve with tortilla chips, crackers, or raw vegetables. Yields 3$^{1}/_{2}$ cups.

Velveeta Fudge

This is a legendary recipe of unknown origin and questionable wisdom that nevertheless racks up about 10,000 hits each year just on the Kraft Web site. We think it's a lot of cyber-rubbernecking.

$^{3}/_{4}$ pound Velveeta or Velveeta Light, cut up
1 cup butter or margarine
6 squares unsweetened baking chocolate
2 tablespoons light corn syrup
2 16-ounce packages powdered sugar
1$^{1}/_{2}$ cups pecans, chopped
1 teaspoon vanilla

Place Velveeta, butter, chocolate, and corn syrup in a large microwavable bowl. Microwave on high for 1 minute. Stir. Microwave an additional minute; remove. Stir until well blended. Gradually add sugar to the mixture, beating with an electric mixer on medium speed until each addition is well blended. Stir in pecans and vanilla.

Pour into greased 9 x 13-inch pan. Smooth top with spatula; cover. Refrigerate 3 hours or until firm. Cut into squares. Makes 3$^{1}/_{2}$ pounds.

Slim Jim
Jerky Ad Campaign Made Meat Snack Sales Snap Back

A recent advertising campaign showed how Slim Jims can wreak havoc in the stomach. It starred a walking strip of sausage (Slim Jim Guy) whose slogan was the mildly obscene, "Eat me!" He got his wish in TV spots that chronicled his adventures inside teenagers.

"Welcome to Timmy's Tummy," a fluffy pink cupcake tells the recently consumed Guy with a welcoming smile in one of the darker ads. "And you are?"

Guy shapes his hand into a gun and pulls the fake trigger. "Leaving," he announces. But not before he clears a path by holding a Twinkie down in some stomach acid.

"Beefy, spicy bully," the cupcake whines.

"You're next, pinky," Guy snarls.

In another ad Slim Jim Guy gives cramps to a kid who goes swimming too soon after eating him.

"You'll thank me," the Guy tells the drowning kid, who is, in fact, saved by a busty, *Baywatch*-style lifeguard. Her reward? A Slim Jim—scented belch in the face.

This, my friends, is one reason meat sticks are the fastest-growing snack in the country.

Advertising for Slim Jim was not always this gross. In fact, the first Slim Jim guy was a gentleman in formalwear who appeared on Slim Jim jars and, later, labels to make the meat snack seem high class. And they *were* high class compared to the other snack that company founder Adolph Levis sold in Philadelphia bars in the 1940s: pigs' feet. Levis hired a local meatpacker to create Slim Jim in response to customer requests for a smaller, neater meat snack and his own interest

Slim Jim Guy sporting his standing-on-end meat stick 'do.

Not to Be Confused With
The thin metal device mechanics (and thieves) use to open locked car doors and the motel and museum promotional brochures found at every tourist information center are also called slim jims because of their skinny designs.

in selling something that had a longer shelf life.

The drawing of the elegant Slim Jim guy had to be scaled down to just a face and top hat when new labeling regulations went into effect in the 1980s—which should give you an idea of the number of ingredients in the original Slim Jim. They included beef, beef organs, corn syrup, 30 secret spices, and lactic acid culture—the latter two accounting for Slim Jim's curious orange color, pungent taste, and eight-month shelf life. Slim Jims lost their organ meat and gained chicken sometime after their 1967 sale to mainstream food maker General Mills.

The brand's first anti-establishment spokesmen were wrestlers.

General Mills also shifted sales from bars to grocery, drug, and convenience stores but assumed the same beefy, blue-collar audience until the brand got its first marketing study, in the late 1980s. Its surprising conclusion? Half the brand's biggest fans were teenage boys for whom the nutritionally naughty snack stick (would you believe 9 grams of fat per .64-ounce serving?) served as the culinary equivalent of nose rings and green hair—in other words, yet another way to tick off Mom.

Slim Jim "courted" teens at a 1999 NBA Hoop-It-Up event.

Advertising has catered to teens ever since: Mid-'90s ads showed World Wrestling Federation star Randy "Macho Man" Savage breaking up a study hall by literally breaking apart a library and razing the set of a languid student production of *Romeo and Juliet*. Although anti-authority and successful, that campaign failed to meet Slim Jim Guy's standard of grossness. Case in point: The Savage ads were backed by NASCAR and extreme sports sponsorships; Slim Jim Guy got a Rebelli-ache Tour of rap and hip-hop acts with such accompanying amusements as a (non-lethal) electric chair and a man who poured beer through his eye socket into his mouth.

Cheez Whiz
Saucy Son of Velveeta

A Teen-age treat that's Frankly Fun!
CARTWHEEL FRANKS

CARTWHEEL FRANKS

Teen-agers, kiddies *and* grown-ups will enjoy these! Cut frank-furters *almost* through, at ½-inch intervals. Broil until they curl into circles. Place on bottom halves of toasted buns. Spoon tangy-tasting Kraft's Cheez Whiz in center of frankfurters. Serve with top bun-halves. The mellow cheddar cheese flavor of popular Cheez Whiz is great with franks!

Cheez Whiz's 1961 solution
to mismatched meat and rolls.

The term *infinity* may have been invented to describe the number of ways you can mess up making a cheese sauce. Dressing up unappealing Brussels sprouts in an enticing orange coating is fraught with the dangers of clumping, curdling, or scalding the cheese you worked so hard to shred. In other words, prior to 1953, the world was in desperate need of Cheez Whiz.

"Project Cheez Whiz," as it was called in the Kraft company newsletter, began in 1951 and lasted almost 18 months. The Kraft laboratory was originally aiming at the then-hot rarebit market (that's rarebit, not rabbit). But anticipating that this cheese-soaked bread dish would soon be about as popular as rabbit, Kraft's sales division asked its researchers to develop an all-purpose cheese sauce instead. They designed a pasteurized product that would keep indefinitely before opening and seasoned it with emulsifiers to prevent the clumping of its many ingredients—including mozzarella, Muenster, and Gouda cheeses, and rarebit ingredients such as mustard and Worcestershire sauce.

"Spread it" on crackers, "spoon it" on macaroni, "heat it" to glamorize leftovers, read one early ad that attempted to explain

Say Cheez Whiz

Saying "cheese" is a time-honored method for producing a smile. But author and executive coach Debra Benton says the best way to achieve that all-important expression of interest in something about which you have none (think Bill Clinton listening to Al Gore) is to say "Cheez Whiz" silently to yourself.

the scope of the product's versatility. "Cheez Whiz has so many uses you'll find yourself dipping into that jar of golden goodness many times a week," predicted another that touted the "elegant" sauce.

But the only serving suggestions to get full-page treatments were macaroni, baked potatoes, Whiz-burgers, and hot dogs. Looking to create "the best burger in the whole universe"? Just cook up a mixture of 1 pound ground beef and 1/3 cup Cheez Whiz and then top it with still more "tantalizing Cheez Whiz." The hot dog ad suggested scoring before boiling so that the dog would curl up to fit on a hamburger bun; you then filled the center hole with Cheez Whiz in a procedure that was "frankly fun."

Great rivers of the bright orange goo flowed freely over American food until it hit the logjam of the natural and gourmet food movements in the late 1960s and early 1970s. Mid-1970s ads picturing Cheez Whiz–Frankfurter Spaghetti and a soupy orange Cheez Whiz Benedict probably did not help Kraft's cause. When Kraft ads of the mid-'80s gamely tried to educate the public about Cheez Whiz's real cheese base, they ran up against formal complaints from Washington, D.C.– and Texas-based consumer groups. A spokesperson for the typically

Coast-to-coast melting pots.

The little glass jars full of ideas.

Cheez Whiz took a road trip across America in 1975 via recipes for a Midwestern casserole, a California quiche, and New England chowder.

crabby D.C.-based Center for Science in the Public Interest called the ads "a deliberate attempt to pass off a cheap, inferior cheese product concocted by food technologists as real cheese."

Cheez Whiz won the battle (it did indeed consist of the required 51 percent cheese to make the ad claim) but had flat sales until one day in 1985, when a Kraft manager with a hankering for nachos got the idea of heating Cheez Whiz in a microwave oven. With a touch of a button, he set in motion Cheez Whiz's rebirth as a "microwave-in-a-minute" sauce used in 28 percent of American households (compared to its historic average of 18 percent).

Since then, the company has attempted to make Whiz keep up with the times. It capitalized on the newer Hispanic and snack food trends with a salsa con queso flavor and a wide-mouth jar for chip dipping. It catered to little kids with a fun squeezable bottle, and to college-aged ones with an ad campaign starring a loud-jacketed Cheesy Guy that embraced the brand's white-trash image. Indeed, Cheez Whiz remains the gold standard for cheese toppings at such temples of American junk foodery as Pat's and Geno's cheesesteaks in Philadelphia and Louis' Lunch (reputedly the birthplace of the hamburger and cheeseburger) in New Haven, Connecticut.

The Commonwealth of Cheez Whiz

Visitors to Puerto Rico expecting to score some empanadilla turnovers, asopao gumbo, fried plantains, or coconut-flavored flan have been understandably surprised to discover firsthand that they are in the Cheez Whiz–eating capital of the world. One favorite PR preparation is an appetizer made by slathering Cheez Whiz on Wonder Bread slices or Ritz Crackers that are then topped with ground Spam (Puerto Ricans' appreciation for the wonders of American processed food not being restricted to Cheez Whiz).

Unauthorized Uses

Not only does that male Heloise-on-speed Joey Green recommend Cheez Whiz as a stain remover, he also titled an entire book of alternative food uses *Clean Your Clothes with Cheez Whiz*.

But at least one Springfield, Illinois, investigative journalist who, per Green's instructions, rubbed Cheez Whiz on a butter grease–stained shirt before washing says she ended up with . . . a butter grease–stained shirt. (The good news: *State Register-Journal* food editor Kathryn Rem's shirt didn't acquire an additional *cheese* grease stain.)

Columbus Dispatch columnist Joe Blundo had more luck with Green's recommendation for using Cheez Whiz as a substitute shaving cream, although he questioned the author's assertion that "Cheez Whiz has no aroma." Based on Blundo's experience, Whiz could reliably serve as an attractive aftershave for Michael Pariza should he wish to continue taking mice out for cheeseburgers.

Not to Be Confused With

The "Cheez Whiz" drag show is held at the Parkside Lounge in New York City every Sunday at 10 P.M.

Mrs. Paul's Fish Sticks
Fish for Catsup Connoisseurs

Babies are born liking sugar—not fish. Fish are so smelly, ugly, and strong tasting, not to mention dangerous (if you miss even one of those bones), it's a wonder anyone thought of cooking them in the first place.

In the first half of the twentieth century, people disguised fish in croquettes, cakes, and loaves, but these more edible fish forms required a lot of time and effort. No wonder, then, that when premade frozen fish sticks debuted in 1952, they were an instant hit. They came in a convenient, predictable rectangular size, and had no bones or haunting fish eyes. Best of all, between the fried coating and ketchup or tartar sauce most people drowned them in, you could hardly even taste the fish.

A 1960 newspaper ad pushed the quality angle.

Fish sticks were a literal godsend for the 30 million U.S. Roman Catholics who were prohibited from eating meat on Fridays or during Lent. In fact, 40 percent of all fish sold in the United States occurred in the seven weeks between Ash Wednesday and Easter, until the Catholic meat-eating prohibition was lifted in 1966. By then, fish sticks were blessed to be on thousands of school lunch menus.

Birds Eye (see page 12) put the first fish sticks in supermarket freezer cases, but it took Mrs. Paul's Kitchens to make them popular. Mrs. Paul's company was started in the mid-1940s by a Philadelphia bar chef with a lousy sense of how many deviled crabs he would sell on any given night. Instead of throwing perfectly good crabs out, Edward Piszek started freezing them and selling them to local supermarkets. Before long, the Mrs. Paul's line also included fried scallops, fish cakes, clam cakes, and fish sticks. It was that last, most downscale, of products that proved to be the company's biggest moneymaker.

In the early days, Piszek and his wife were a sales team: Piszek would make the sale;

Mrs. Paul's Philadelphia fish stick factory line in 1989.

then his wife, posing as Mrs. Average Housewife, would enter the store and begin extolling Mrs. Paul's products' virtues within earshot of the manager. Other relatives acted as reinforcements, buying products at new stores to artificially inflate demand.

Piszek also thumbed his nose at the then-standard food industry practice of having a single distributor handle a single company's products in each local market. Instead, he signed up

Pop Question

Q: Why fish sticks? Why not fish rounds or triangles?

A: Because fish arrives at fish stick factories in long, frozen blocks, cutting them into rectangular shapes creates the least waste, according to Ed Piszek's son, Bill. The beauty of fish sticks for most manufacturers, of course, is that they can be made of up to 60 percent batter or breading as well as minced unmentionables from pollack, cod, or whiting (hence their status in this chapter featuring food recyclables). Mrs. Paul's Fish Sticks, however, are made from whole fillets and are therefore practically gourmet.

Spinoff

Mrs. Paul's Chicken Sticks were an early 1980s sales *Titanic*. But fish tenders—a breaded fish product based on the popular fast food chicken nuggets—hauled in big money for frozen fish makers in the late '90s.

HELLO There was a Mrs. Paul (several actually), but she had almost nothing to do with the fried fish that bears her name. Ed Piszek called his company Mrs. Paul's Kitchens only to placate an early business partner named John Paul. Paul was then the company chef, but both partners thought their housewife customers would relate better to a cook of their own sex.

Piszek bought out Paul in 1951 and in turn sold out to Campbell's Soup in 1982, but he has remained active as one of America's most prominent Polish philanthropists. A $1-million donation he made to combat tuberculosis in his parents' native land in 1963 virtually wiped out a disease that was then raging out of control. In 1971 he invested half that for an ad campaign aimed at combating the scourge of Polish jokes from American popular culture (in part by publicizing the accomplishments of such famous Poles as Chopin, Joseph Conrad, and Copernicus). In 1980 he shipped 250 trailers of fish cakes to fortify Polish workers protesting against their Communist government.

All this put Piszek on a first-name basis with Lech Walesa and that other John Paul—the one whose followers were responsible for many of Mrs. Paul's early fish stick sales.

everyone he could get and backed up his distribution network with an aggressive program of national advertising, including one campaign featuring an on-his-way-down Orson Welles.

Fish sticks have been headed in a similar direction recently due to health concerns about fried foods, the popularity of the microwave (which is ill suited to them), and the increasing popularity of fresh fish (due in part, ironically enough, to training-wheel products like fish sticks).

Bus shelters were an unusual and unusually successful advertising venue for Mrs. Paul's in the 1950s.

Ore-Ida Tater Tots
Small Fries

Purple ketchup, mystery-flavor Kool-Aid, and game-festooned Lunchables are all trying much too hard. Such obvious pandering is a turnoff even to kids, and the main reason these companies have to keep coming up with new gimmicks to keep up sales.

Other than the name (which, I'll grant you, is tot-centric), there is nothing on the Tater Tots package either now or when it was invented that would identify it as a kids' food. Kids are just naturally drawn to Tater Tots' small size, lob-friendly shape, and bland taste—especially when they're sitting next to chicken nuggets or a hamburger.

This, apparently, is the recipe for a kids' food that lasts and lasts. And yet kids were the furthest thing from frozen French fry manufacturer F. Nephi Grigg's mind when he created Tater Tots in 1953. Grigg, in fact, was trying to figure out what to do with all the little pieces of potato left over after cutting up a potato into French fry–sized sticks. He had been selling them as cattle feed, but that was practically giving them away. He hit upon the idea of chopping up the potato slivers, adding flour and

The original Tater Tots box proudly displayed its origins.

seasoning, then pushing the potato mash through some holes in a three-quarter-inch piece of plywood and slicing off pieces of what came out the other side. It was the birth of the Tater Tot.

Ore-Ida's first and largest potato-processing facility is located in Oregon, right near the border of Idaho, where F. Nephi Grigg got many of his potatoes—thus its company name combining the first few letters of both states.

That name in turn inspired one of the world's corniest advertising slogans: "When it's Ore-Ida, it's All Righta." Its long-lasting success is proof positive that deep down Americans are still basically a bunch of hicks.

Today Grigg's Ore-Ida company is a division of ketchup-maker Heinz and America's largest maker of frozen potato products. Tater Tot sales are second only to the Golden Crinkles French Fries of which they are the byproduct. They're still made in the same Ontario, Oregon, factory where they were invented and in much the same way (although a steel wheel has replaced the plywood tot former).

Even with all the shiny new equipment, Heinz research and development manager Joe DeStephano says Tater Tots are a challenge to make. One problem is getting potato black spots out of the slivers. Another is keeping the potato mash from falling apart on its way to the fryalator. DeStephano calls his solutions to these problems trade secrets.

DeStephano says the company has yet to figure out a use for the bits of fried Tater Tots that drop off along the way, but he's open to any suggestions that measure up to F. Nephi Grigg's original breakthrough.

The Crunchier Side of Ted Kaczynski

One of the more puzzling discoveries from Unabomber Ted Kaczynski's Montana shack, given his back-to-nature lifestyle and hatred of technology: an empty Tater Tots box. "He must have wanted a side dish with his rabbit," an Ore-Ida spokesman ventured at the time.

The original Tot maker.

Not to Be Confused With

The slothful young counterparts to adult couch potatoes are frequently called tater tots.

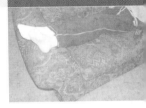

Tater Tots Casserole

This Midwestern potluck favorite (and traditions like it) help to explain how *A Prairie Home Companion* has been able to keep going for more than a quarter century.

1 pound ground beef
1 medium onion, chopped
1 10½-ounce can cream of mushroom soup
Salt and pepper to taste
1 32-ounce bag frozen Tater Tots
1 cup Velveeta, grated

Preheat oven to 375°F. Grease a 2-quart casserole dish. Cook beef and onions over medium-high heat in a skillet until beef loses its red color. Spoon off excess fat. Mix in soup and season with salt and pepper. Pour mixture into casserole dish and top with Tater Tots. Sprinkle with Velveeta. Bake 45 minutes or until center is hot and bubbly. Serves 4 to 5.

Useless Statistics

According to Ore-Ida's 1994 Tater Tots Survey, the average human mouth can hold seven Tater Tots (providing they're not too hot). Slightly more than half of the Tater Tots–consuming population eats them with a fork. About 4 percent of the American population claims to have eaten 10,000 or more Tater Tots.

Chapter 5

MARKETING MARVELS

When you get down to essentials, food is basically just different arrangements of starch, fat, sugar, and salt. Why pick one preservative-laden, sugar-blasted snack cake over another? Why would anyone choose to become one with a clam-tomato juice?

We do it because we've been brainwashed to believe they're something more than just starch, fat, sugar, and salt. We do it because sometimes these ad and marketing folks' ideas are even better than the food itself.

Jell-O
There's Always Room for Colored and Flavored Boiled Animal Hide

Wild Strawberry

It looks like plastic, acts like rubber, and changes from solid to liquid on the ride down to your stomach.

It has assumed the guises of wrestling mat, life-sized nude political sculpture, adult alcohol shots, gummy candy-like Jigglers, colorful cubes pelted around school cafeterias or tentatively consumed in the sickroom, and showpiece molds stuffed with fruit, nuts, miniature marshmallows, and any number of real or fake dairy products. In fact, it's almost as hard to escape Jell-O in North America as it is hard to find it anywhere else in the world.

Could it be because Jell-O displays so many of the elements of the American character that foreigners love to hate? It is bright, brash, sweet, unsophisticated, lighthearted, and lightweight. It's also democratic. There are many gourmet brands of coffee and beer and cookies but none of flavored gelatin desserts.

Jell-O actually democratized gelatin. Before it, gelatin dessert–making was a daylong, multi-step ordeal that involved straining and skimming (of water from boiling calves' feet—more than that, you don't want to know).

Lights, Camera, Gel!

Jell-O's most famous scene on stage or screen occurs in *Animal House*, where John Belushi provokes a cafeteria food fight by inelegantly inhaling several green squares of the stuff. But Jell-O also helped part the Red Sea in the 1923 version of *The Ten Commandments* (fleeing actors were superimposed between two undulating halves of a sliced Jell-O mold). Jell-O was also the SPCA-approved "paint" used on the horse of many colors in 1939's *The Wizard of Oz*.

America's most famous dessert

JELL-O
Six
Delicious
Pure Fruit
Flavors

The
Quality
is Always
the Same

THE JELL-O COMPANY Inc. LE ROY, NEW YORK

In the 1920s, Jell-O ads featured gallery-quality still life paintings.

Jell-O creator Pearle Wait.

No one without servants would attempt it. That's why gelatin was a sign of wealth in the Victorian era, much like driving a Lexus or wearing a Rolex watch is today.

Gelatin convenience products began appearing in stores at the end of the nineteenth century. These were unflavored sheets or powders made in much the same way as home gelatin (except for a last drying step) and designed mainly for use in cooking and baking. In 1897 Pearle Wait of LeRoy, New York, was the first to add coloring and flavoring to gelatin powder to create a stand-alone dessert mix his wife dubbed Jell-O. How and why he did this is not known. What is known is that Jell-O was America's first dessert mix of any kind.

Jell-O may jiggle, but at first, Jell-O sales did not move much at all. After only two years, Wait unloaded the product on fellow LeRoy businessman Orator Woodward. The problem, Jell-O "stepfather" Woodward eventually figured out, was that women were used to cooking from scratch. They didn't know what to do with a food that didn't require recipes. So Woodward gave them some.

That first Jell-O recipe booklet—distributed door-to-door in 1902 by salesmen in horse-drawn wagons—marked the beginning of a vast and diverse recipe library that now includes the classic Under-the-Sea salad (lime Jell-O, pears, and cream cheese), the delicious Parfait Pie (Jell-O and vanilla ice cream), the showy Jell-O stained glass (different colored cubes of Jell-O set in Cool Whip), the magical Jell-O poke cake (Jell-O poured on baked cake), and the weird Red Hot Salad

Collectors' pins featuring an old Jell-O delivery truck, an early box, and the original advertising spokesgirl.

Finally, an Explanation for the Popularity of Yanni

Perhaps you've heard the expression, "He has Jell-O for brains." Well, it's apparently true of us all. Dr. Adrian R. M. Upton of McMaster University Medical Centre in Ontario, Canada, proved it by hooking up an EEG machine to a mound of lime Jell-O and comparing the same test's readouts from healthy human beings. They were almost identical.

Upton's experiment actually had the serious aim of showing how electrical interference from hospital equipment could produce readings on the EEGs of patients who were as lifeless as a bowl of Jell-O, but it has resulted in much ribbing. Among other things, colleagues have asked him to consult on several "critical" pudding cases.

A Jell-O box, circa 1923.

(cherry Jell-O, applesauce, and Red Hot candies). In the '50s and '60s especially, there wasn't much a woman could do that would be more impressive than turning out an unbroken gelatin salad mold.

But who has time to make elaborate Jell-O dishes nowadays? Only retirees and full-time homemakers. Not surprisingly, the Jell-O sales capital of America today is Salt Lake City, Utah, a city filled with stay-at-home Mormon moms. (No wonder, too, that a pin depicting a bowl of lime gelatin proved to be one of the most popular souvenirs of the 2002 Salt Lake City Winter Olympics.) Jell-O sales peaked in the late 1960s, but the company has stemmed further sales losses with the introduction of the Jell-O Jigglers recipe and ready-to-eat varieties.

But You Can Still Buy Mixed Fruit

Among the Jell-O varieties not in the current U.S. or Canadian flavor line-up (perhaps for good reason): celery, mixed vegetable, coffee, cola, bubble gum, cinnamon, and Italian salad.

Jell-O 1,2

Of all the many Jell-O spinoff products none is more beloved than Jell-O 1,2,3. After being whipped then placed in the refrigerator, this food-cum-science-experiment produced a gelatin bottom, a chiffon middle, and a Cool Whip–like top. It debuted in 1969 but was discontinued; it was reintroduced in 1988 and discontinued again in 1996. Until it comes back, Jell-O 1,2,3 fans can nurse their whiplash with this do-it-yourself two-tiered Jell-O dessert recipe.

³/₄ cup boiling water
1 3-ounce package Jell-O gelatin, any flavor
¹/₂ cup cold water
Ice cubes
¹/₂ cup whipped cream or Cool Whip

Pour boiling water into blender. Add gelatin. Cover and blend at low speed until gelatin is completely dissolved, about 30 seconds. Combine cold water and ice cubes to make 1¹/₄ cups. Add to gelatin mixture and stir until ice is partially melted. Add whipped topping and blend at high speed for 30 seconds. Pour into dessert glasses. Chill about 30 minutes. Dessert layers as it chills. Serves 4.

Jell-O, The New Dessert, pleases all the family. Four flavors: Lemon, Orange, Raspberry and Strawberry. At your grocers. 10cts. Try it to-day.

Parkay
The Spread That Sasses Back

The Parkay product line now includes light sticks (above), and calcium, squeeze, and spray varieties (facing page, far right).

What a Difference 70 Years Makes
In the early twentieth century, some dairy industry–protectionist state laws (see opposite page) required margarine to be dyed pink to make it as unappetizing as possible.

In 2001 Parkay came out with a new shocking pink–colored Fun Squeeze spread for kids.

A bite of Imperial margarine on toast suddenly and magically produced an Imperial crown. Mother Nature got angry about being fooled into thinking Chiffon margarine was butter.

Commodity products like margarine have inspired some of America's best ads. It's understandable: Why else choose any one margarine over another? But Parkay's wise-guy talking tub is one of the most memorable margarine ad campaigns of all.

"Butter," the tub would blurt out to some kids at the kitchen table or unwitting suburbanites in the dairy aisle.

"Parkay," the people would shoot back with a mild scold.

Then they'd take their first bite of the stuff.

"Butter," they'd assent, to which the Parkay tub would mischievously retort, "Par-kayyy!"

Parkay was America's third-best-selling margarine tub before these arguments were televised in 1973. Less than a year later, it was No. 1.

And so the gag continued for more than 20 years, more or less unchanged except for the occasional addition of a real or imagined celebrity (Edgar Bergen and Charlie McCarthy, football's Deacon Jones, actors playing Laurel and Hardy, comic Al Franken, and even Santa Claus). In 1999 the Parkay ads showed the tub on the couch talking out his delusional thinking.

Parkay's ad silence of several years might have made some think the therapy worked. Instead it turned out that the tub was just gearing up for a new and even more annoying phase. In 2002 Parkay announced that 15,000 Parkay tubs would come equipped with motion-activated computer chips so that they could enter into the Eternal Butter-Parkay Debate with

After 30 years, the Parkay tub still says "Butter."

real supermarket shoppers. "The label says Parkay, the flavor says butter," the tubs would blurt out to any shopper who passed by. The carnival barker approach was justified, a Parkay executive at ConAgra Foods argued: Statistics showed that 70 percent of shoppers decide what brand of margarine they're going to buy while in the store. ConAgra sweetened the sales pitch by having one of the computer-equipped tubs tell its purchaser they had won a $10,000 prize.

Others saw this promotion as evidence that Parkay officials were having as much trouble distinguishing between funny and not funny as consumers had between butter and margarine. This rule of thumb might help: Funny is a margarine tub talking to someone else; not funny is when it argues with you.

When Margarine Was an Illegal Substance

State liquor laws are eccentric and annoying. But they're nothing compared to what margarine lovers had to put up with until the middle of the last century. The blend of oil and water we know as margarine was invented by a French chemist in 1869 to remedy a French butter shortage and debuted in the United States shortly afterward as a dangerous drug. The protectionist dairy industry was behind this designation, as well as the federal Margarine Act of 1886, which required anyone who made, distributed, or sold margarine to be licensed; it also imposed a federal tax of 2 cents a pound (later raised to 20 cents). By 1902, 32 states had laws that also prohibited manufacturers from making margarine look anything like butter (thereby giving housewives the messy chore of working yellow dye into the unbuttery-looking, unappetizing white blocks). And so a margarine black market sprung up to rival moonshine's during Prohibition.

Butter shortages during both World Wars increased margarine's popularity and shortened consumers' patience with the butter protectionists. In 1949 housewives dressed in suits, gloves, and bonnets marched on Washington to protest the federal restrictions, which were repealed in 1950. The dairy state of Wisconsin was the last to drop a state ban against the sale of yellow margarine in 1967—and only after Wisconsin state senator Gordon Roseleip, the law's chief proponent, failed a blind butter-margarine taste test. His daughter later confessed that the senator's family had switched to margarine years before without his knowledge.

In any case, U.S. margarine consumption doubled between 1950 and 1970 and is now three times that of butter. The dairy lobby apparently had good reason to be afraid.

Clamato
"It sure doesn't taste like clam juice!"

For years V8 marketers have struggled to explain how and why their vegetable juice blend is different and better than plainer (and cheaper) tomato juice, their chief solution being ads where someone slaps himself on the forehead and exclaims, "I could've had a V8!"

But that challenge pales compared to what competitor Clamato is up against: convincing people that a clam and tomato juice drink is a tasty treat.

An ad touting the Clamato Bloody Caesar as the natural successor to the Bloody Mary.

At Clamato-maker Mott's, the problem has long been known as "the clam barrier." Just why California-based executives at the predecessor Duffy-Mott company put clam juice in their new tomato drink, and what's probably even worse, in its name, is a mystery to Clamato's current handlers. What they will say is that Americans' distaste for clamminess would have sunk the drink into the drink along with its clams long ago had a Canadian bartender at an Italian restaurant not come up with a recipe for a Bloody Mary–like concoction inspired by a red clam sauce pasta dish. Clamato soon became a standard shortcut ingredient to make that drink.

As If Clamato Weren't Already Weird Enough
Mexicans' and Dominicans' favorite way to consume Clamato is in a half-and-half concoction with beer in a taste treat known as red beer.

"Clamato and beer. Make one," commands this ad aimed at the only demographic group that might actually consider doing it (Spanish-speaking Mexicans and Dominicans).

Today this Clamato-based Bloody Caesar drink is as much a part of Canadian identity as Mounties or Molson. As a result, despite having only a little more than one-tenth the population of the United States, Canada almost matches its southern neighbor in Clamato sales.

Many of Clamato's U.S. sales can be attributed to Hispanics. Although they always drank more Clamato than Anglos did, it was only in the late '90s that Mott's began studying Hispanic Clamato consumption habits. (This was about the same time that a last, desperate effort to get Anglos to drink it—with an ad campaign that denied its clam identity—failed.) Hispanic women in focus groups told Mott's that they used Clamato to cook pork chops, cure hangovers, and get "energized"—at which point the women would turn red and begin giggling. Among Hispanics with Caribbean roots, Clamato (and most other shellfish-based foods) is considered an aphrodisiac.

Bloody Caesar

6 ounces Clamato
1½ ounces vodka
1 dash Tabasco
1 dash Worcestershire sauce

1 dash horseradish
1 wedge lime
1 stalk celery

Combine ingredients through horseradish and put in shaker glass with ice. Shake, strain, and serve in glass with lime and celery garnish. Serves 1.

Kellogg's Pop-Tarts
Granddad of Grab 'n Go

America has a dog food to thank for its favorite breakfast pastry.

Pop-Tarts was a people food byproduct of General Foods scientists' attempts to create a moist dog food patty that wouldn't spoil. After the success of Gaines Burgers in the early '60s, the company's Post cereal division decided to borrow the technology to create a jelly-filled pastry that would

Rosy-cheeked spokestoaster Milton gives the 1973 flavor countdown.

remain edible (at least to some people) for up to nine months. The secret to extending the products' shelf life was keeping the water activity low so that it prevented the growth of bacteria. They called that first toaster pastry "Post Country Squares" and introduced it to the press in 1964, much to the chagrin of executives at archrival Kellogg.

"My first thought was that it would be highly unlikely any youngster who had one of those for breakfast would be eating a bowl of cereal too," recalls Bill LaMothe, then Kellogg's product development VP. Not knowing much about pastry, Kellogg's sought help from a nearby Keebler cookie plant with relevant experience making fig bar cookies.

Within four months Kellogg's had a competitive toaster

Pop (-Tarts) Question I

Q: If a single Pop-Tart is one serving, why do Pop-Tarts come two to a wrapper?

A: Because once that package is opened, only someone with an iron will can eat just one. And Kellogg's wants you to finish the box fast, natch.

But economics of a different kind were behind the initial decision. "The packaging equipment was expensive," recalled Bill Post, who was the manager at the plant that produced the first Pop-Tarts. "To package them singly would have required twice as many machines. Kellogg's didn't want to invest in a lot of machines until they knew how it would sell."

pastry product that adult focus groups trashed. The complaints ranged from "the pastry is too hard" to "it doesn't fit in my toaster" to "can a kid cook one of these without killing himself?" But Keebler plant manager Bill Post's kids not only survived their preview pastry toasting sessions, they loved the new product. Post was always bringing home new cookies and crackers that his kids "usually turned their noses up at. But they asked me to bring home more of those fruit scones." And so Pop-Tarts discovered its kids' market.

Kellogg's courted these kids by running ads featuring cartoon toaster Milton on *Huckleberry Hound, Yogi Bear,* and *My Favorite Martian* (and in more recent years, by tie-ins with everyone from the Backstreet Boys to Batman). The addition of frosting in 1967 almost doubled sales overnight. Sprinkles followed soon thereafter. Today there are Pop-Tarts with blue frosting and shark-shaped candy sprinkles, and others that change color when toasted.

More than 70 percent of all Pop-Tarts are eaten toasted. In fact, "warmth" is one of the top reasons people say they like them. In the days before Hot Pockets, the novelty of using the toaster for something besides toast was also part of Pop-Tarts' appeal. Then there was the name, which, although originally intended to refer only to the way they pop out of the toaster, perfectly and permanently pegged the sturdy, bespeckled slabs as edible "pop" culture. (Although Pop-Tarts

Milton teamed up with a mixer named Fred to produce creme-filled Pop-Tarts in 1973.

Weapons of Edible Destruction

In 2001 Pop-Tarts popped up in almost as many news reports as toasters.

In August it was the news that a Pennsylvania woman was suing Pop-Tarts maker Kellogg's over a $100,000 fire in her home, one of more than a dozen Pop-Tart–related blazes reported to the U.S. Consumer Product Safety Commission over the course of 10 years.

A few months later came the more benign but equally odd report that the U.S. military was air-dropping Pop-Tarts on Afghanistan as part of humanitarian food packages.

The combination prompted more than one news writer to wonder whether the product wasn't some kind of Trojan Horse intended to cause the Taliban and perhaps even Osama bin Laden himself to go up in flames with their breakfast.

Incidentally, a chemistry professor who took a blowtorch to a Pop-Tart in order to intelligently comment on the Pop-Tart fires says the pastry's sugar filling does make it more flammable than bread, but he conjectured that an irresponsible person and a defective toaster are probably also required.

Q: Why is Kellogg's so skimpy with Pop-Tarts' fruit filling?

A: Saving money on pricey preserves may be a side benefit, but the real reason, according to former Kellogg manager Bill Post, is that too much filling makes the pastry tops explode and could also make the Pop-Tarts too heavy for toasters (2 ounces is the max for most models).

Incidentally, the perception of a plentiful fruit filling (or lack thereof) prompted the company to stop scoring Pop-Tarts in half on a diagonal, as they were for the first year or two. This made them easy to break in half, but the dough stitching made it harder to see the fruit preserves they did contain. And what consumers can't see, they think doesn't exist.

may have triumphed over Country Squares mainly because of an aggressive distribution push, Country Squares certainly wasn't helped by a name that suggested a country bumpkin.)

Pop-Tarts were also clearly a lot more convenient than homemade or bakery pastries—in part because they still tasted good (or at least the same) for months instead of days after purchase. And that was back when people still had time to go to the bakery.

No wonder Pop-Tarts sell even better today than in the '60s. No wonder, too, that Bill LaMothe went on to become company chairman. Per his prediction, sales of Kellogg's Pop-Tarts now beat any of the company's cereals.

"Filling" a Need for Variety

The first Pop-Tart flavors were strawberry, blueberry, brown sugar cinnamon, and apple-currant—the latter being very quickly changed to apple-berry when it became apparent that few Americans knew what currants were.

The brown sugar cinnamon flavor was suggested by U.S. sales chief Mard Leaver. Former Kellogg VP Bill LaMothe remembers the skeptical looks around the table when Leaver waxed rhapsodic about the cinnamon sugar toast he enjoyed as a kid. "But he was going to be a key guy in making Pop-Tarts a success, so we asked our research guys to take a look at it." Brown sugar cinnamon jumped to the top of the Pop-Tarts sales charts almost as soon as they were introduced, and they have remained there to this day.

Flavor flops include chocolate-peppermint, cherry chip, and frosted peanut butter and jelly.

The many faces of Pop-Tarts include (from left to right) 1994's Pop-Tarts Crunch cereal, the original scored Pop-Tarts, Frosted Pop-Tarts, and Low Fat Chocolate Fudge with bilingual packaging (sold in French Canada).

SpaghettiOs
Who Says Spaghetti Should Be Straight?

Winding spaghetti on fork tines is one of those life skills—like riding a bicycle or tying shoes—you don't just pop out of the womb knowing. So anyone who sets a toddler down in front of a bowl of sauce-soaked spaghetti should do so with fear, trembling, and a bottle of Mr. Clean at the ready.

At least that was the messy situation until 1965, when Franco-American decided to create a more kid-friendly spaghetti for the legions of post-war babies. What law said spaghetti could only come in long, unwieldy strands?

After some discussion of spacemen, star, and cowboy shapes, and witnessing a company chef serve up a dish of sliced elbow macaroni and sauce, the Franco-American marketing geniuses decided on four different-sized circles, in the mushy consistency that kids prefer. The tomato sauce was also sweeter and cheesier than the sauce in any of their canned pastas for adults.

They put the pasta in a can decorated with a childish

The first SpaghettiOs print ads touted its kid-friendliness.

Why Not Simply Little, Littler, Still Littler, and Littlest?

The official names of the four different-sized rings in SpaghettiOs brand pasta are (from largest to smallest): Ditalini, ditali, tubetti, and tubetini.

Meat You Can't Eat

These days Franco-American frequently enters into licensing agreements to make SpaghettiOs-style canned pastas featuring cartoon character shapes. In 1995, such a deal produced Shnookums & Meat Shaped Pasta with Tomato & Cheese Sauce, based on a Disney cartoon about a cat named Shnookums and a dog named Meat. In other words, it was a product called Shnookums & Meat that contained no meat.

Franco-American could have avoided any possible confusion by just making a Shnookums & Meat with pasta and meatballs. But then they would have missed out on sales from the majority of young consumers who prefer plain pasta. Instead, they chose to make a plain product with the world's weirdest label disclaimer: "Meat is a character developed by Buena Vista Television. THERE IS NO MEAT IN THIS PRODUCT."

drawing of a face (featuring two pasta rings for eyes) and launched an advertising campaign that addressed both kid and parent audiences. To kids, a "spaghetti that you eat with a spoon" was both novel and naughty—like eating peas on a knife. The "uh, oh" in the SpaghettiOs song chorus reinforced this appealing idea.

Parents' concerns about spaghetti's messiness were addressed by the mom who appeared at the very end of the TV ad to enthuse, "It's the greatest invention since the napkin!"

Within weeks Franco-American factories were in overdrive trying to keep up with demand beyond their wildest pasta-shape imaginings.

Soon there were SpaghettiOs pasta with meatballs or franks, and in shapes like teddy bears, Garfield, and in 1992, Waldo (in this case, spelled WaldO), of hidden picture book fame. In 1993 the pasta ring itself became a cartoon figure when TheO (The "O"— get it?) took the place of the old label smiley face.

As the first main dish food product designed specifically for kids, SpaghettiOs is also indirectly responsible for the creation and success of Lunchables meal kits, Kids Cuisine frozen entrées, and many other kid food products that are probably even more worthy of the SpaghettiOs brand's cautionary "uh, oh."

"It's the greatest invention since the napkin!"

SPAGHETTIOs

SpaghettiOs drives home its neatness point on a napkin.

In 1994 SpaghettiOs used a comic book to introduce consumers to its new cartoon spokespasta, TheO.

The French Connection

The Franco-American brand originated in 1887 when French émigré Alphonse Biardot opened a commercial kitchen in Jersey City, New Jersey, to market products that would introduce Americans to gourmet foods from his native land. Among his earliest products was a line of six truffled game pâtés.

By 1920 Biardot had expanded his offerings to include fancy Italian dishes, including a canned Spaghetti à la Milanaise. SpaghettiOs is that product's blue-collar descendant.

The neat round spa- ghet- ti you can eat with a spoon

Uh Oh Spa- ghet- ti Os.

He Sang Pasta's Praises

Remember Jimmie Rodgers? We don't either. But he was apparently the Britney Spears of the late '50s and early '60s, producing such hit songs as "Kisses Sweeter Than Wine," "Turn Around," and "Oh-Oh, I'm Falling in Love Again" (a possible inspiration for Spears's "Oops! I Did It Again"?).

That's why when Franco-American approached him about singing the jingle for their new ad for SpaghettiOs pasta in 1965,

Rodgers suggested inserting the phrase "Oh-Oh" (or, as he ended up singing it, "Uh-Oh") into the song's chorus.

The voice of this teen idol and the catchy tune had a powerful effect on both sales and people's consciousness. Even today baby boomers who have forgotten everything they learned in college can sing the whole thing.

Little Debbie Snack Cakes
Cheaper by the Dozen

Pop Question

Q: Why is one of the Little Debbie snack cakes called Devil Squares? Is the company involved in satanic worship?

A: Hardly. In fact, the McKee family are such devoted Seventh-Day Adventists that all the Little Debbie factories are still on the Sabbath. The adult Debra McKee herself once took a leave from the company to help promote a Christian TV station. The devil in the Devil Square name refers to their sinfully delicious devil's food cake base.

"**L**et them eat cake," Marie Antoinette reportedly said of some breadless subjects in 1789, thus ensuring her spot in history as a symbol of royal insensitivity. If only she had lived in the time of Little Debbie snack cakes, she would merely have been seen as an eighteenth-century Suze Orman.

That's because it's possible to buy a box of 12 Little Debbie Swiss Cake Rolls for as little as $1.09 in twenty-first-century money. That's about 1,620 units of pure energy (i.e., calories) for less than the cost of a cup of coffee. It's also about a third the cost of a box of Yodels, a similar snack made by Little Debbie competitor Drake.

How can Little Debbie be so cheap?

It's mainly due to a savvy combination of low-moisture ingredients and natural preservatives that make Twinkies seem fresh-out-of-the-oven by comparison and give the company more than a month to get their cakes sold via a network of cheaper, independent non-union distributors. (Competitors Hostess and Tasty Baking, by contrast, pay their own truck drivers to stock store shelves with fresh product nearly every day.)

This is not to say the company is anti-labor. Little Debbie–maker McKee Foods gives its employees a generous yearly bonus and provided

The evolution of the McKee multipack, from the late 1950s . . .

A box of the popular oatmeal pies after it acquired the familiar full-color Little Debbie drawing.

profit sharing and a fitness center (to work off all those assembly line rejects?) decades before modern high-tech companies. And McKee stock is actually worth something: The company has posted profits every year since 1972. There is also no mandatory retirement age. In fact, until he finally decided to retire in the summer of 2003, Little Debbie's guru of new product ideas was 90-year-old Cliff Dildy.

Company founder O. D. McKee began his snack food career selling Virginia Dare baked goods out of the back of the family car in Chattanooga, Tennessee, in 1933. By 1934 O. D. had purchased the first of two Jack's Cookie companies he would own before launching McKee in 1957. A number of popular Little Debbie treats, including oatmeal pies, got their start at one or the other Jack's. But the McKee company's real success began with the intro-

. . . to 1960, when the snacks were first sold under the Little Debbie name and drawing.

Big Debbie Is One Smart Cookie

The supermarket aisles rival beauty pageants for female airheads: the Sunbeam Girl, the Sunkist Raisin Maiden, and the Land O' Lakes Indian Princess among them. Debbie McKee is one notable exception. Although her three-year-old face smiles from every Little Debbie snack cake box, her adult one just about never appears in public. That might not be such a bad thing. If she did, she'd probably put everyone to sleep with talk of horizontal flowpack wrapping machines and just-in-time delivery—her areas of expertise in her very important and unfluffy job as the McKee company's director of manufacturing.

duction of economical family packs under granddaughter Debbie's name. (McKee had already innovated the first multipack in the snack food industry a few years earlier.) An artist's rendering of a studio portrait of Debbie in a straw cowgirl hat, complete with the crease from where she had stepped on it, became the brand's logo.

Achingly sweet, dime-store cheap, and as off-trend with modern eating habits as that portrait, Little Debbie products are nevertheless enormously popular, accounting for seven of ten of America's best-selling snack cakes.

The real Little Debbie feeds her public.

Green Giant Canned Peas
Yucking It Up in the Valley

A canned pea is a canned pea is a canned pea—that is, they're nearly always grayish and mushy. The fact that Americans buy more Green Giant canned peas than any other brand can be laid squarely at the very large, green leaf–clad feet of the Green Giant, an animated amalgamation of Saturn (god of the Harvest), Jack (of the Beanstalk), Paul Bunyan, and Santa Claus.

Surprisingly, the Giant was not a marketing brainchild but the answer to a legal problem. An executive of the Minnesota Valley Canning Company wanted to begin canning a new variety of unusually large peas under the name Green Giant. But being descriptive, the name was not trademarkable. Their lawyer suggested pairing the name with a picture that could be legally protected.

Sculpture of the original non-green Green Giant.

The first giant belied his *Grimm's Fairy Tales* inspiration. Debuting on can labels in 1925, he scowled, was nearly dwarfed by the pea pod cradled in his arms, and wasn't even green. It took advertising wunderkind Leo Burnett to make the Green Giant big and jolly. Through almost 20 years of print ads set in the Minnesota River Valley (but known as "the Valley of the Jolly Green Giant"), Burnett so successfully sold the public on this American agricultural god and his superior vegetables that, in 1950, the Minnesota Valley Canning Company officially changed its name to Green Giant.

The Dog Ate These, Too

Cell phones, PDAs, and instant messaging have changed the way kids work and play. But when it comes to trying to avoid eating vegetables, modern kids are sticking to such time-honored methods as pushing their vegetables around on their plates so it looks like there's less (40 percent), feeding them to the dog (16 percent), or giving them to a more passive or vegetable-friendly kid (12 percent)—this according to a telephone survey of American moms conducted for Green Giant by Market Facts Inc. in 1999.

Television almost slayed the Giant. Lumbering across the screen for the first time in 1959, the rubber-skinned puppet looked like a creature from a low-budget monster movie. Ad and company executives alike agreed that he shouldn't walk or talk ("ho, ho, ho" excepted) on TV. This obviously had a freezer-like effect on Burnett copywriters' creativity. (Do you think there'd be all those Santa TV specials—not to mention all those cards and snow globes—if all St. Nick did was stand there with arms akimbo and say, "Ho, ho, ho"?)

Little Green Sprout

Enter the Little Green Sprout, a cute, childlike cartoon brussels sprout who could walk and talk without causing undo alarm and who, with his collection of animal friends, upstaged the Giant everywhere

The Green Giant's half-century graphic evolution: 1928   1930

except on the vegetable cans and boxes. W. C. Fields had advised against working with kids and animals but failed to warn against precocious brussels sprouts. In any case, the Giant's nice-guy persona didn't really allow for firing the little guy or serving him from a bulging can, if you get my ho, ho, ho drift.

The Valley disappeared from ads entirely in the '90s in favor of live-action advertising for the company's rapidly expanding array of frozen vegetable medleys and meal starter kits. Could there also have been a feeling that the big green lug sales pitch had become a bit too, well, corny?

Perhaps. But the witty print ads that accompanied the Giant's return to advertising in 1999 (reminiscent of the Altoids Mint ads also devised by Burnett) were as cool as his frozen veggies. "I've been digging up dirt for years," read one ad in the *National Enquirer,* while another in *People* magazine's Best-Dressed issue referenced his leafy tunic: "When you dress like this, you BETTER eat your vegetables."

This 55-foot-tall Green Giant statue looks over pea and corn fields in Blue Earth, Minnesota. In winter he gets a scarf; during motorcycle rally season, a leather vest and bandana.

1936   1960   1978

Swanson TV Dinners
How One Box Led to Another

Dollar stores are filled with failed attempts to trade on the popularity of some celebrity or hot trend. Frozen dinners are one of America's only long-running sales-through-association stories. Their success is all the more remarkable considering the trio of inspiration behind them: the boob tube, airline food, and some decaying turkey meat.

November 1951 was a particularly warm month

"My boys are crazy about Swanson TV Dinners!" —SAYS MRS. T. M. CARROLL, JR., 5500 RIVER FOREST DRIVE, ARLINGTON, JACKSONVILLE

In this early ad testimonial, Mrs. T. M. Carroll said she never had to call her boys to dinner twice when she served Swanson.

in the United States, and following Thanksgiving, turkey processing giant Swanson was left with 10 refrigerator railcars filled with turkeys that remained unsold because people had decided to eat something lighter for the holiday. The turkeys had to travel back and forth from Omaha to the East Coast, Swanson's warehouses being already as stuffed as a Thanksgiving bird.

Not long before this, however, Swanson salesman Gerry Thomas had met a package salesman who showed him a tray his company was designing to serve food on airplanes. This was also a time when crowds clogged the sidewalks in front of store window displays featuring the new "picture radios."

Starring Swanson
In the film *Play It Again, Sam,* empty TV dinner trays litter the apartment of the newly single Woody Allen. Allen's retort when a friend asks if that's all he can cook: "Who bothers to cook 'em? I suck 'em frozen."

Speaking of Suckas
In the early 2000s, nostalgic trend-setters could order old-fashioned Swanson TV dinners at several hipster restaurants (including New York's ike and San Francisco's Butter) at $6 a pop.

Speed of preparation was the message of this mid-'50s Swanson ad.

TV dinners quite naturally teamed with a popular TV show for one of its first premiums.

Thomas put the two ideas together and suggested his company freeze the surplus turkey and sell it alongside potatoes and vegetables in compartmentalized trays called TV dinners. They would link the magic of a world-at-your-fingertips entertainment medium with the miracle of a complete meal that required no preparation.

Frozen dinners had previously been sold in a limited way with limited success. Swanson itself was already making frozen potpies. But with home freezers then almost as novel as TVs, the Swanson brothers agreed to only a modest initial order of 5,000 turkey-sweet potatoes-cornbread stuffing dinners. They came packaged in a box that looked like a television set with a show about

The Real Reason Frozen Dinners Were So Hot?

In his book *What Were They Thinking?* Bob McMath talks about a promotion that ad man Chuck Mittelstadt dreamt up to encourage consumers to try the new Swanson TV dinners: Buy one and get a dollar back.

It was a great idea when the dinners sold for $1.09, as they did initially. But it became a problem when supermarkets began using the exciting new product as a loss leader and prices dropped to as low as 59 cents. In effect Swanson was paying consumers 50 cents (almost $5 in today's money) to try their product—an offer that Mittelstadt may have personally needed to take advantage of when he lost his job over this little miscalculation.

Unauthorized Uses

In the early days TV dinners were prized as much for their aluminum trays as for the food they contained. Men used them to store nails and screws; women used them to corral buttons or cut them into shiny Christmas tree ornaments.

Swanson switched to plastic trays in 1986 in a bow to the popularity of the microwave. Today the only place you can still find the aluminum trays is next to Fonzie's jacket in the Smithsonian or in cupboards of 80-year-olds who've never been able to bring themselves to throw them away.

the dinner playing. Preparation time was 45 minutes.

Neither Thomas nor the Swansons had envisioned the dinners actually being eaten in front of the TV. But TV dinners were something early TV owners could prepare for their many new "friends"

The infamous banana-flavored fried chicken. (Note the yellow cover color.)

without missing one minute of Milton Berle. They could even be eaten in a darkened room, the compartments located the food so predictably. And for those who couldn't afford a TV, serving TV dinners was the next coolest thing.

After the novelty of TV wore off, the dinners became something to eat on Mom's night off. Even if they couldn't say so, most kids actually preferred the TV dinners to Mom's home cooking. They liked the way the trays kept the food from running together and the chance to choose what they were going to eat. After the dessert compartment

Swanson introduced TV dinners to the trade via this 1954 ad in *Frozen Food Age*.

Trust
Swanson
to be first
again!

NEW

Swanson TV Brand

Loin of Pork Dinner

Loin of pork was typical of the upscale or special occasion meats in the early TV dinners.

debuted, there was no better way to measure a kid's character than to watch the order in which she consumed the different courses.

The dinners also marked the beginning of the end of American families sitting down at a table and eating the same meal together.

New idea from Swanson!

Hungry-Man Dinners

The second helping of meat is already in.

After years of complaints from men about skimpy portions, Swanson bowed the hearty-sized Hungry-Man line in 1972.

The company's second TV dinner variety was banana-flavored fried chicken—although the banana flavor was unintentional. It turned out that a banana-derived yellow dye used to decorate the box was leaching into the food. Although most consumers complained, Swanson ended up unloading the whole lot of "banana" fried chicken to a food chain in Florida whose customers couldn't get enough.

Roast beef and haddock, the third and fourth dinner varieties, debuted in the mid-'50s. Former Swanson salesman Gerry Thomas blames lingering resentment about World War II for the flop of a sauerbraten-Bavarian red cabbage-spaetzle dinner the company introduced in the late 1950s.

When diet frozen entrées were all the rage in the 1980s, Swanson promoted its contrarian line of Hungry-Man really fatty and salty dinners. In 2002 they pushed the concept into On-Cor territory with Hungry-Man XXL, featuring 1½ pounds of meat and potatoes (and no icky vegetables).

Hawaiian Punch
The Drink with the Refreshingly Hostile Commercial

The pugnacious Punchy.

A Hawaiian bearing a cooling glass of red fruit drink and a big smile approaches the prototypical tourist with a generous offer: "How about a nice Hawaiian Punch?"

"Sure," the tourist guy with the flowered shirt and the big droopy eyes would inevitably reply as the Hawaiian—aptly named Punchy—wound up to smack the poor schlub in the kisser.

In sophistication, this bit of comic business ranks right up there with flatulence humor and Prince Albert-in-a-can phone pranks. Hilarious if you're 6, and one of the major reasons (along with sugar) Hawaiian Punch has always been a "hit" with kids.

The drink that caused the equally aptly named Oaf so much suffering was invented by a couple of chemists in Fullerton, California, in the 1930s. A. W. Leo and Tom Yates had been trying to distill real fruit juices into fruit concentrates when one or both of them combined juices from several tropical fruits into a yellow-hued fruit punch concentrate they called Leo's Hawaiian Punch. They initially sold the punch only to soda fountains as a sherbet and drink base or ice cream topping. It was only after company treasurer Reuben P. Hughes bought out Leo and Yates in 1946 that the name lost its Leo and the drink gained some water, its fruit-juicy red color, and a clunky metal can container.

In the '50s the drink rode the wave of popularity for all things Hawaiian or sort of Hawaiian. (The drink was at least as authentic as Trader Vics, *South Pacific,* and Elvis's *Blue Hawaii,* which is to say, not very.) And when the light from America's patio tiki torches began to fade, the brand was saved by the now-famous ad campaign.

Pop Question

Q: What are the "seven natural fruit juices" the Hawaiian Punch ads were always crowing about?

A: Nowadays, pineapple, passion fruit, orange, papaya, guava, pear, and apple. (A 1970s formulation contained grapefruit and apricot instead of the pear and apple.) Apples in Hawaii? Not in any beach party movie we've ever seen, but there are lots at Mott's, Hawaiian Punch's current corporate manager.

Hawaiian Punch Apple Sauce was the inevitable result of applesauce maker Mott's 1999 acquisition of the brand.

After paying the Atherton-Privett agency to create this Polynesian Punch-and-Judy routine in 1962, Hughes's Pacific Hawaiian Products Company had very little money left to air it. So it bought a slot on the dirt-cheap *Tonight Show* with Jack Paar, "a late-night sophisticated show and

Unauthorized Use

Sickened by the idea of drinking a syrupy sweet kid's punch? At least as many people say that Hawaiian Punch soothes an upset stomach. The July 2001 issue of *Prevention* magazine theorizes this is due to its sugar, an ingredient Hawaiian Punch shares with cola syrup, another popular nausea remedy. But unlike cola, Hawaiian Punch doesn't contain caffeine and so won't keep you from getting the sleep an ailing body needs.

absolutely the wrong place to advertise a household product bought by mothers for kids," says John Urie, one of the ad men involved. Fortunately for the company, Paar was so startled by Punchy's blithe hostility that he asked the control room to run the ad again. For free. "Three days after that, you couldn't buy a can of Hawaiian Punch in New York," Urie recalled.

The punning and pummeling continued for almost 15 years. Punchy got a punchline only in the late '70s ad campaign featuring Donny and Marie Osmond, notable chiefly for the way Marie's on-screen hairstyle instantly changed from straight to curly to held-back-with-an-Indian-headband (although what this had to do with Hawaiian Punch is one of advertising history's great mysteries). In the 1980s Punchy was abandoned entirely in favor of beach scenes of frolicking teens. Pacifist moms probably hoped Punchy had spent his hiatus in anger therapy. But when Punchy returned in 1990 he was still cracking noses and cracking kids up.

There's a lot more competition in non-carbonated drinks these days, but Hawaiian Punch's handlers are wise enough to realize (in the words of a 1991 ad slogan) that "Nothing else has the Punch."

Hawaiian Punch was once a bottled drink concentrate. Ready-to-drink cans debuted in 1950.

Permissions and Trademarks

Grateful acknowledgment is made to the following for permission to use trademarks, and recipes and artwork featuring them:

Birds Eye Foods, Inc. for its trademark, Birds Eye.

Kraft Foods, Inc., for CHEEZ WHIZ® Process Cheese Sauce, COOL WHIP® Whipped Topping, EASY CHEESE® Pasteurized Process Cheese Spread, JELL-O® Gelatin, KOOL-AID® Soft Drink Mix, KRAFT® Macaroni & Cheese Dinner, MINUTE® Rice, PHILADELPHIA® Cream Cheese, SANKA® Decaffeinated Coffee, SHAKE 'N BAKE® Seasoning Mix, TANG® Drink Mix, and VELVEETA® Pasteurized Prepared Cheese Product, all registered trademarks of Kraft Foods Holdings, Inc., Artwork courtesy Kraft Foods except JELL-O art on pages 114 and 115 (bottom), which is courtesy LeRoy Historical Society (photo on page 114 bottom taken by Gennelle Thurman).

On-Cor Frozen Foods, Inc., for On-Cor.

General Mills for its trademarks Pillsbury, Poppin' Fresh, Doughboy, Green Giant, Sprout, Bac-Os, Betty Crocker, Potato Buds, Bisquick, Hamburger Helper, Tuna Helper, Taco Bake, and Helping Hand. Photo on page 131 (right) courtesy Blue Earth (Minn.) Area Chamber of Commerce.

Durkee-Mower, Inc., for Marshmallow Fluff.

Hormel Foods Corporation for DINTY MOORE Beef Stew and SPAM. DINTY MOORE, SPAM, and all SPAM-derived terms are registered trademarks of Hormel Foods, LCC.

ConAgra Brands, Inc. for Jiffy Pop Popcorn, Reddi-wip, PAM, Parkay, and Slim Jim. Photographs © ConAgra Brands, Inc. There is no financial or legal association between ConAgra Brands, Inc., and the author or publisher of this book. Page 57 PAM photos courtesy Robert Meyerhoff.

Procter & Gamble Company for Pringles.

Unilever Bestfoods affiliated companies for its registered trademarks I Can't Believe It's Not Butter! and Lipton Cup-a-Soup. Page 59 photo courtesy Al Carlson.

Cumberland Packing Corp., Brooklyn, N.Y., for its registered trademark, Sweet 'N Low.

Interstate Brands West Corporation for Wonder Bread and Twinkies.

The Coca-Cola Company and Minute Maid for Minute Maid. Artwork courtesy Paul L. Sjolin.

Beer Nuts, Inc., for Beer Nuts.

Nestlé for Carnation Instant Breakfast, Carnation Instant Nonfat Dry Milk, and Coffee-mate materials © Nestlé and used with permission. Nestlé, Carnation, and Coffee-mate are registered trademarks of Nestlé S.A.

Aurora Foods for Mrs. Paul's. Pages 106 and 108 photos courtesy Piszek family. Page 107 photo courtesy Temple University Libraries, Urban Archives, Philadelphia, Pa.

The H.J. Heinz Company for Ore-Ida Tater Tots. Artwork courtesy Heinz.

Mott's Inc., for Hawaiian Punch and Clamato.

Kellogg's and Pop-Tarts are registered trademarks of Kellogg Company.

Campbell Soup Company for SpaghettiOs. Trademarks, artwork, advertising, and promotional materials related to the SPAGHETTIOS brand are the intellectual property of Campbell Soup Company or its subsidiaries, and are used herein by permission. There is no financial or legal association between Campbell Soup Company and the author or publisher of this book.

McKee Foods Corp. for Little Debbie. Photos courtesy McKee Foods Archives.

Pinnacle Foods Corporation for Swanson, which is a registered trademark of CSC Brands, Inc.

Index

Acknowledgments

I don't particularly recommend writing a book while making an out-of-state move and beginning a new job. But if you want to give it a try I hope you have as much help as I did.

This principally came from the following food brand experts. If there is anything interesting here, it's because of information, photos, and/or recipes supplied by Kara R. Mallory, Meri Harris, Gene Lifka, and Shawn Radford at Hormel Foods Corporation; John W. Faulkner and Beth Jolly at Campbell Soup Company; Tonia Hyatt at Procter & Gamble; Chris Curran and Judy Klym for Mott's; Roz O'Hearn, Marie Olson, and Tricia Bowles of Nestlé; Michael Drinkard of Cumberland Packing Corp.; Stan Osman and Mike Redd of Interstate Brands Corporation; Kara Krehbiel and Derek Hall of Boasberg/ Wheeler Communications; Marlene Johnson, Peg Ilkka, Heidi Geller, Kim Harbinson, Shelly Dvorak, and Anitra Budd of General Mills, Inc.; Donald Durkee of Durkee-Mower, Inc.; Becky Niiya, Kay Carpenter, Karen Johnston, Scott Lerner, John Timmons, Tony Balk, Pam Gaik, Angela Joyner, Ellen Grau, and Teresa Paulsen of ConAgra Foods; Dana Emery of Unilever; Michelle Luechtefeld and Eric Grosgogeat of Aurora Foods; Liz Barrett, Lauren Winer, and Susan Kaminski of Dome Communications; Lisa Garvick of Blue Earth Area Chamber of Commerce; Neil Mermelstein of *Food Technology*; Meredith Myers of the National Potato Promotion Board; Don Odiorne of the Idaho Potato Commission; food technology consultant Sara Risch of Chicago; Mili De Brown of Mi Caminito Puerto Rico Inc. (www.MiCaminito.com); Manfred Kroger of Penn State; Cindy Shirk of Beer Nuts; Alan Bloomfield and Hayward Blake for On-Cor; Bea Slizewski of Birds Eye; Laura Hernandez and Barbara Hodgson of Rogers & Associates; Jenny Enochson of Kellogg Company; Erica Tarlowe and John Kroeger for Swanson; Ray Crockett and Paul L. Sjolin of Minute Maid; Robin Teets of Heinz; Lynne Belluscio of the LeRoy Historical Society; Teresa Kreutzer-Hodson of The Hastings Museum; Andrew Smith (for valuable information about Jiffy Pop in his book, *Popped Culture*); also Patti Sullivan, Henry Constantino, Anne Choi, Bonnie Tandy Leblang, Alicia Comstock Arter, James Tills, Bill Post, Bill LaMothe, Bill Piszek, Scott Evans,

Alexander Pack, Toni Lee, Blaine Hess, Lance Tibbetts, Valerie Richardson, Judith Meyerhoff Yale, Linda Levine, Byron Lapin, Ramon and Charles Sanna, Gyneth Mayer, and George Brown of the Wyandot Popcorn Museum.

Special thanks are due those who came through for me not once but twice (because of a computer hard-drive crash), including Yasmeen Muqtasid and Lisbeth Armentano of Nestlé, John McIndoe of Information Resources Inc., Jennifer May of Heinz, and Robert Meyerhoff; the much-put-upon (and appreciated!) archivists Jane McClure (of Nestlé), Katie Dishman (of General Mills), and Becky Haglund Tousey (of Kraft); and Renee Zahery (also of Kraft), who served as traffic controller for 12 of this book's most fascinating brands.

In whipping up this information into palatable form, I'm grateful for the guidance and support of the smart, patient, and professional team at Quirk headed by Dave Borgenicht, Mindy Brown, and Michael Rogalski; and for punching up by a comedy writer (Douglas Wyman) who doubles as a wonderful brother.

And no acknowledgments by me would be complete without a nod to the two Phils: Greenvall, the proprietor of my own personal sound-side Yaddo, and Blumenkrantz, who got the brunt of my stress and neglect. Now that the book is done, I promise to start unpacking the boxes.

Table of Equivalents

U.S.	Metric
1/4 teaspoon	1.25 milliliters
1/2 teaspoon	2.5 milliliters
1 teaspoon	5 milliliters
1 tablespoon	15 milliliters
1 fluid ounce	30 milliliters
1/4 cup	60 milliliters
1/3 cup	80 milliliters
1/2 cup	120 milliliters
1 cup	240 milliliters
1 pint	480 milliliters
1 quart	960 milliliters
1 gallon	3.84 milliliters
1 ounce	28 grams
1 pound	454 grams
2.2 pounds	1 kilogram

Oven Temperatures

Degrees Fahrenheit	Degrees Centigrade
200	93
250	120
275	140
300	150
325	165
350	175
375	190
400	200
450	230